BRUCE
surgeon
soldier
statesman
sonofa

B R U C E

surgeon
soldier
statesman
sonofa

by CHARLES GODFREY

ISBN 0-9684226-1-6

Codam Publishers, RR1 Madoc, Ontario K0K 2K0

Printed and bound in Canada by Gandalf Graphics

Contents

Special Abbreviations

BMJ	*British Medical Journal*
CD	Canadian Doctor
Chorley	Chorley Park, residence of Lieutenant-Governor, Ontario
CJMS	*Canadian Journal of Medical Science*
CJPH	*Canadian Journal of Public Health*
CMA	Canadian Medical Association
CMAJ	*Canadian Medical Association Journal*
CP	Canadian Pacific
MP	Member of Parliament
OCTRF	Ontario Cancer Treatment and Research Foundation
OMA	Ontario Medical Association
PHJ	*Public Health Journal*
SW	Social Work
the General	Toronto General Hospital
the House	House of Commons, Ottawa
TSM	Toronto School of Medicine
U of T	University of Toronto

Special Abbreviations (Military)

ADMS	Assistant Director Medical Services
CAMC	Canadian Army Medical Corps
CEF	Canadian Expeditionary Force
CCS	Casualty Clearing Station
CO	Commanding Officer
DMS	Director Medical Services
DDMS	Deputy Director Medical Services
FO	Foreign Office, London
GOC	General Officer Commanding
NCO	Non-commissioned Officer
RAF	Royal Air Force
RAMC	Royal Army Medical Corps
VAD	Voluntary Aid Division
WW1	World War 1914-18
WW2	World War 1939-45

Acknowledgements

I am delighted to acknowledge
the pleasure of many hours of fascinating discussion
with numerous people who have assisted me.
Of course, they are not responsible for any written word.

Mr. Paul Arculus, Professor Michael Bliss, Mr. David Bruce,
Dr. Dale Dotten, Dr. Jackie Duffin, Dr. G. Hart,
Lieutenant Colonel and Mrs. S. Hughes,
Dr. W. Prendergrast, Mr. Peter Ridout, Dr. H. A. Smythe,
Dr. A. Squires, Dr. R. Volpe, Dr. Neil Watters,
and, most influentially, Mr. Maxwell Bruce,
were all interested and helpful in the project.

Dr. T. Dukes expertly assisted me with his research
at Queen's University,
where we were made welcome by Archivist Don Richan.
The staff at the Archives of Ontario,
the National Archives, the University of Toronto,
and The House of Lords, London, England,
were most obliging.
Ms. Andrea Gallagher Ellis was kind enough
to copy-edit my manuscript
and Ms. Anne-Amor Nepomuceno carried the bulk of the typing.
Cover Design by gogogirlie GRAPHIKS

The Board of Directors of The Wellesley Central Hospital
Corporation, especially Ms. L. Burnham and Dennis Magill,
were enthusiastic backers of this project,
and I acknowledge, with thanks,
the financial support of the Corporation.

CHARLES GODFREY

BRUCE
surgeon, soldier, statesman, sonofa

CHAPTER 1

The Making of a Surgeon

The band of the 34th Battalion never sounded louder. Bugles cut through the summer heat as the locomotive of the Port Whitby and Port Perry Railroad chugged into the station. And there, on that July day in 1880, emerging from swirling, sooty smoke, was the tall lank figure of the Father of Confederation, John A. Macdonald. A great shout erupted from the sun-drenched crowd, drowning out the commands of Captain Samuel Sharpe, as he called the troops to attention and then to march down Queen Street, past Aaron Ross's new grain elevator, the offices of The Observer and The Standard (one for each political party), around the corner by the Presbyterian Church fronted by the Sons of Temperance Choir (mixed), and past Allison's drugstore. The parade of democrats, two-wheeled gig carts, and heavy wagons, loaded with red-faced blue Tories, finally drew up at the platform in the town square, which was jammed with supporters and old friends. It was a bully day for Port Perry.

John A. bounded up the steps to greet and shake hands with two old timers who were veterans of the 1866 Fenian Raids and MP Peter Christie and Militia Captain Sam Hughes, who had rushed over from Victoria for the event. Hughes never lost an opportunity to hear — or give — a speech.

It was also important to have a word, and slap the back of the man who had led the parade riding a white horse, that stout Conservative and good Orangeman — Stewart Bruce. He had left his farm to bring his wife, Isabella, and their children, Robert, Albert, Herbert, Minnie, and Rupert, to see the Great One, who had come to give a speech, tell some stories, and hold court in the tap-room of Sinclair's Hotel. Bruce, being a Temperance man, chose to picnick with his family at the lakeside, before taking their wagon back to the farm, about a mile past the school.

This school was the pride of the neighbourhood since being recognized by the Department of Education as the best in the province. It was headed by Dugald McBride, M.A., who taught classics and imprinted the love of literature on the tabulae rasa who crowded his class. Bruce had moved his farm from Blackstock to Mt. Albert to be near the school. There was a strong mathematics teacher and Miss Gordon, sister of a Member of Parliament, who insisted on proper composition and grammar.

Herbert, the third son, enjoyed his lessons and haunted the small library of the Mechanics Institute, which provided other than course books. Although he spent many hours reading, there was his share of farm chores, especially at harvest time when each family in the neighbourhood pooled labour to bring in the crops. They used a Massey reaper, but it was necessary for six men and boys to follow, rake the grain and bind the sheaves. The hard work was matched by hard play. In the good weather it was lacrosse or field days — but never on Sunday. Herbert, because of his speed, became adept at both, and there was always a swim in Scugog to end the day. The lake also served in the winters as a rink for shinny or a course for cutter racing. Stewart Bruce's farming was moderately successful, but there was little money for higher education.

Having passed his junior matriculation in 1884, Herbert tried to fulfill his ambition to become a doctor — a lifelong dream, but he was too young to enter medical school. On the advice of the family doctor, John H. Sangster, he apprenticed to C. E. Allison, one of the two druggists in town. Sangster usually made and sold his pills and potions, but there was still room for dispensing druggists. He became notable later in the decade, when he organized Ontario doctors into a Medical Defence Association which objected to the $1 membership fee levied by the Ontario College of Physicians. Many rural practitioners joined the protest, but the movement petered out after Sangster died in 1903. However, his legacy of demanding an accounting from institutions in authority and of mounting a strong process of dissatisfaction, persisted.

Bruce's apprenticeship paid $1 a week with a bonus of enlightening experience in meeting and sometimes advising the sick. It strengthened his desire to enter the Toronto School of Medicine (TSM), but also impressed upon him the gullibility of the public which heeded the advice of an ignorant farmboy. Allison's drugstore had one of the few telephones in town and was connected to another in Whitby, a few miles away, where another student, Llewellyn Barker, worked. The two had many long conversations, without charge, as the two telephones were local offices of the Telephone Company. Barker preceded Bruce into medical school and later served as a private instructor in anatomy to a small group, including Bruce.

This duo of friends was joined at sporting events and socials by Haymar Greenwood from Whitby, who sometimes brought his attractive sister Florence to the occasions. But with his drugstore duties, sports and playing the pipe organ, Bruce had only minimal time for socials. After two years in Allison's store he read an advertisement of an opening at a pharmacy in Toronto, owned by Dr. Jehu Ogden. As it provided more experience, plus $5 a week, and was close to the medical school, Bruce applied and was accepted.

Leaving Port Perry was difficult, because of the many friends he had made in the area including a young Sam McLaughlin, who was talking about automobiles. All the Bruce family were still working on the farm, and had not begun to branch out across Canada. Albert would remain and take over the farm on his father's death in 1912. Robert would move to Toronto and become a hardware merchant; Minnie married a clergyman and moved to British Columbia, and Rupert became a successful industrialist in Toronto.

Ogden's pharmacy was at Bathurst and Queen streets and there was a different type of client from the stable rural community of Port Perry. The customers were mostly recently arrived immigrants who stayed for a few months in the Kensington area and then moved on to better housing and more space in newer areas of the expanding city.

Jehu's brother Uzziel was on the teaching faculty of the University of Toronto Medical Faculty and noted the enthusiasm and intelligence of the young apprentice, so that, in 1888, Bruce was admitted to the largest school of medicine in the province. In truth, he could have applied to Trinity College, the Anglican medical school, but careful consideration of the facilities offered by the University of Toronto (U of T), and the Ogden connection, persuaded him that U of T was the better choice. Some of these decisions may have stemmed from the recent course of medical history in Toronto.

In 1887 after 40 years of proprietary medical schools, the TSM was reconstituted as the University of Toronto Medical Faculty. This was accomplished against the opposition of Dr. W. O. Geikie of Trinity who, following the teachings of Dr. John Rolph, objected strenuously to the spending of public money to educate doctors who would generate a good income. Pitted against this opinion, which continued over many years, was William Mulock (later Sir), a lawyer and member of the Senate of the U of T, who took a particular interest in medical matters. Mulock was convinced that it was more reasonable to spend money to educate doctors to prevent diseases, than to allow the diseases to happen. Prevention justified funding doctors' education with public money. Mulock was an assertive, canny man who dominated the U of T Medical Faculty for many years.

The Dean of Medicine was William T. Aikins who had previously directed the TSM. He was a respected, skilful surgeon who used Bruce as an assistant on many occasions before his graduation. Although Aikins did not subscribe fully to Joseph Lister's antisepsis procedures, he was one of the first to stress cleanliness and avoidance of transferring disease from one patient to another.

It was an exhilarating time to be a medical student. A fresh wind was blowing through the halls of learning as the discoveries of Louis Pasteur became more widespread, giving fresh hope to the sick that there was reasonable chance of recovering, and to the doctor that he could do more than offer sympathy and a collection of unproven or ineffective medications. Indeed, science had arrived in medicine with the work of Sir Michael Foster in physiology, Friedrich

Loffler in diphtheria, and Patrick Manson who had shown that insects could cause disease — even malaria. The world was in wonderment from Robert Koch's announcement of the causative bacillus of cholera in 1884, which was followed by the discovery of the tubercle bacillus.

The incorporation of the TSM into the University meant much more facility for teaching of the sciences, such as chemistry, physics, and sanitation, which were now seen as vital components of medical practice. Professor Ramsay Wright had begun courses in microscopy for the identification of bacteria, and conferences that co-related clinical histories, pathological findings, and the results of treatment were becoming common.

The buildings of the TSM at River and Carlton streets were still used for anatomy teaching. They were convenient to the Toronto General Hospital, where demonstration clinics were given by surgeons such as George Peters, W. P. Caven and the Dean. Bedside teaching, however, was still not common. Biology lectures were given at the Biology Building on University grounds which meant a two-mile walk for students. It was worth the effort to hear the stimulating lectures by Wright. All this worked up a good appetite which was partially satisfied by the three hearty meals that Bruce had per day at a boarding house at Gerrard and Parliament streets. For sleeping and a cramped space for study, he shared a room, and bed, with fellow student Clarence Starr. This arrangement was changed the next year when sixteen of the class rented a house in Cabbagetown, saving money by doing their own housekeeping. Although the cooking may have suffered, there was enhancement of discussion and more opportunities for co-operative learning. The only break in Bruce's routine was when his mother came to Toronto for treatment of a swollen, hot, painful knee. She had heard of a Christian Scientist who was expert in treating this problem. Bruce discovered that the cure consisted of waving of hands about the area plus appeals to self-cure. Mother was dispatched back to Dr. Sangster in Port Perry. Bruce, who had always been an outstanding student, flourished and in his final year (1892) won the gold medal. He graduated and received the Bachelor of Medicine degree from the Chancellor, The Honourable Edward Blake, and William Mulock was on the platform.

During the next year Bruce was one of the eight chosen house surgeons at the General, which was a signal honour as his class had approximately sixty students and there were another sixty applicants from Trinity. He rotated through each service of medicine, obstetrics, and surgery, and also had some pediatrics. His time on medicine was spent chiefly in treating typhoid fever and tuberculosis. Obstetrics was absorbing and he examined patients before they were seen by Dr. James F. W. Ross, the expert gynecologist, who, although kind, demanded clear and specific diagnoses. Ross had kept an index of 2850 deliveries he had made and recorded all factors including the position of the foetus, how the delivery was made, and the outcome. Bruce became adept at diagnosing placenta previa by placing his stethoscope in the vagina and listening for the rush of blood — a bruit — which signaled a dangerous situation. His astuteness was noted by Ross, and also by Dr. Adam Wright, Professor of Pediatrics and Secretary of the Faculty.

In the same year Ramsay Wright was funded by Mulock to attend a special course in Germany given by Koch to study tuberculosis and a possible vaccine.

Mulock, although a lawyer, had a high interest in medical matters and accompanied Wright. Unfortunately, the "cure" was not successful; however, there were other enormous medical successes about that time. Dr. George Murray reported a successful treatment of myxoedema by injecting a compound of animal thyroid. W. M. Bayliss and E. H. Starling proposed and demonstrated the action of secretin, derived from ground-up stomach tissue, which when injected into an animal caused an increased flow of pancreatic juices. This was the first of the chemical messengers, or hormones. And before Bruce's graduation, von Behring and O. Minkowski had shown that the removal of the pancreas could cause diabetes in a dog.

In spite of these dramatic "breakthroughs" Bruce was taken by the work of surgeon George Peters, the only Canadian to have qualified in the Royal College of Surgeons in England. He was the most competent of the surgical staff and not even I. H. Cameron, the professor who succeeded W. T. Aikins as dean, would operate unless Peters assisted. His example steered Bruce to his post-graduate thesis on intestinal anastamosis. In this work Bruce replaced the "Murphy button" made of bone, designed by J. B. Murphy, of Chicago, to hold the two ends of a severed intestine together until healing took place. Bruce successfully used small plates made from a turnip for the same purpose. His rationale was that by the time the intestine had healed and pulled together, the vegetable would disintegrate. It was much better than the button, which sometimes caused ulcerations in the healing stage.

His thesis was accepted and he was awarded the Doctor of Medicine, MD, by the Dean and Mulock, and once again won a medal for the best original paper.

Bruce was now an expert anatomist. His excellence in the subject resulted from the special tuition he had received from Barker, three years his senior, who had managed to work his way through medical school. However, Bruce lacked both surgical experience and money. While casting about for a place to set up practice, good fortune arrived in an envelope asking if he would be interested in accepting the job of ship's surgeon on the Canadian Pacific's, *Empress of India*, a new 5900-ton liner.

The opportunity was seized and he was soon underway from Vancouver to Hong Kong. His duties were not onerous and, in addition to the $60 per month salary, he could charge patients for any illness, except sea-sickness. It was a good experience and during the voyage he performed his first appendectomy. Actually, he had never been at the operating table for such an operation. He had assisted Aikins in removing the end of the humerus and ulna, in an operation performed in a private house. At that time, the procedure took approximately six hours and Bruce noted that Aikins would "park his knife, between his teeth." The operators stopped for lunch, while the patient was "kept under" by the anaesthetist. However, the only time he had observed an appendectomy was from the operating room gallery at the General.

Before Bruce graduated, there were few doctors in North America who specialized in surgery. It was a bloody business and few dared to open the body cavities, whether chest or abdomen, and certainly not the head, except in cases of extreme urgency or accidental injury. For example, when President James Garfield was shot by a single bullet, which entered the chest about the third rib, the only procedure carried out by his attending physician was to probe the opening with a finger. There was no question of infection. By the tenth day the wound was discharging "healthy pus" and on the fortieth day the president died. Part of this reluctance to separate medicine from surgery was a long-standing suspicion of those who specialized. It was necessary for the physician to be a generalist. Only travelling lithotomists, eye doctors, clap doctors, and quacks practised their trade in one specific area. The first chest surgery was performed by Rudolph Matas of New Orleans in the 1880's, who used a special tube to maintain breathing while the patient underwent the procedure. Local anaesthesia using cocaine, which obviated the need for maintaining a breathing passage, was not available until Carl Koller's discovery in 1884. William S. Halstead, the famous Hopkins surgeon, used Koller's findings with cocaine to experiment upon himself and acquired a habit. But there was little surgery of the abdomen until that done by Harvey Cushing of Baltimore. Henry James Bigelow had excised the hip joint in the 1880's and Samuel David Gross of Jefferson Medical School along with Nicholas Senn, pioneered surgery of the intestines. With the discoveries of Lister, it was possible by 1890 to speak of aseptic surgery, which meant that surgeons, such as Murphy of Northwestern University of Chicago, could operate on arteries and do end-to-end resections.

A pain in the belly, particularly in the lower right area, was usually diagnosed as typhilitis, which was presumed to be an inflammation of a blind pouch in the intestine called the cecum. However, Reginald Heber Fitz proved this not to be the case in the paper he published in 1886, which analysed 460 cases of abdominal distress and showed that in the vast majority this resulted from an inflammation of the appendix. His work was succeeded by that of Charles McBurney in 1899, which demonstrated McBurney's point as an inflammation of the appendix, and could be diagnosed by palpation over a specific area of the lower right abdomen.

This information was known to Bruce and had been supplemented by the fact that in Fergus, Ontario, in 1883, Abraham Groves performed an appendectomy on a patient on a kitchen table with relief of the patient's distress. Groves, who practised his own particular type of antisepsis, taught at the TSM that he boiled his instruments and washed out the abdominal cavity with hot water.

All this lore was of great use to Bruce as he carried out the operation on an impromptu operating table in a pitching hull. The procedure was a double success. First, the patient recovered, and second, he was the first human on whom Bruce had operated. The fee for such an operation was usually $100, although there was a sliding scale to match the economic status of the patient. This revenue was in addition to another source of income. The Canadian Pacific would not transport coffins. However, many elderly Chinese, wishing to be buried in their homeland, took passage on the line and died en route. When this happened Bruce was employed to embalm the body. He was paid $40 for this service, with some subtractions for canvas shrouding etc. etc. The body was allowed to continue to China, where the corpse was buried as desired.

While Bruce enjoyed these trips, and was also accumulating money for his post-graduate courses, he felt that he had to quit after four round-trips and seek other employment, possibly to practise in Toronto. However on the last leg from Hong Kong, he was approached by a man who was escorting a young Scot back to Edinburgh. The Gael was a severe alcoholic who could not resist the smell of a cork, and it was the charge of his companion to insure that he arrived home in as reasonable shape as possible. That escort had become fed up with the difficulty of riding herd on the whisky swiller and suggested to Bruce that he should take over the job. The offer was sweetened by a first-class passage from Canada to Glasgow. The payment was more than adequate.

Bruce accepted this windfall and, after a harrowing trip, was able to make his way to London and finally to begin his post-graduate course. He applied at University College, presented his credentials to the Secretary of The Royal College, took a room in Brunswick Square, and began another year of intensive learning. Having little excess money, socializing was at a minimum, although he did manage an occasional gallery seat in the theatre, through the friendship of a fellow boarder, who was the manager. But one social event was notable: Dr. Starr Jamieson, who raided the Transvaal and was a precipitator of the Boer War, returned to University College and was given a luncheon by the medical class.

Another remarkable experience, which cost nothing, was the day Bruce spent in the courtroom of Oscar Wilde — an event on which he ruminated for years, in face of the changing morality of the world.

To qualify to become a Fellow of the Royal College of Surgeons, it was necessary to pass the examination of the Royal College of Physicians which took six months, and then take a membership in the College of Surgeons. Having passed these hurdles he obtained several locums to increase his cash, and his practice skills.

The primary examination for the Fellowship consisted of anatomy, comparative anatomy, physiology, and histology. One-third of the candidates succeeded. The lectures of Wright and Barker were paying off. His learning experience during the next six months was with the greats of the United Kingdom — Victor Horsley, Arthur Barker, Christopher Heath, Richard Godlee, a nephew of Lister, and Albert Carless. The last offered special evening tuition, which was expensive but returned great value. Horsley offered lunch which upset Mrs. Horsley who, unwarned, had prepared only two chops.

His tuition included visits to all the great London hospitals, including St. Bartholomews, and Middlesex, where John Bland-Sutton demonstrated surgery on both humans and animals, as he was curator of the London Zoo. Professor Leonard Hill was already establishing an outstanding reputation in physiology, and his knowledge provided an added ability to take the examination. Finally in the autumn of 1896, Bruce achieved his objective and was admitted to the degree of Fellow of The Royal College of Surgeons.

A celebration was in order. From druggist's apprentice to Fellow of the most prestigious medical society in less than ten years! But, aside from his parchment, there were no pounds in his pocket. Drawing on his previous contacts and experience with Canadian Pacific, he applied to the Orient Steamship Company as a surgeon on a Mediterranean cruise ship. It would recoup some of his savings and provide an opportunity to see a good part of Europe. Besides, there were well-to-do passengers who were anxious to visit Gibraltar, Malta, Jerusalem, and Rome.

In the Holy City there arose a dilemma, when he joined a group which had an audience with Leo XII. His Holiness remarked, "You come from Canada?"

before Bruce kissed the ring. He never told his Protestant, Orange Order father of that event.

The cruise included visits to many biblical sites before returning to Gibraltar. There, under the Mediterranean blue sky, he received a bolt which started him on his professional career. A cable from William Mulock, Vice-Chancellor, informed Herbert A. Bruce that he had been appointed Associate Professor of the Faculty of Medicine, University of Toronto, and when could he come?

The offer was tempting, in reality the prize for which he had striven over ten years. On the other hand, there were two alluring positions in England. After weighing opportunities, possibilities of future advancement, patriotism to Canada and Ontario, the decision was made to return to Ontario.

It was opportune that the invitation had not been made when he arrived in Toronto, but was an accepted contract. This became quite apparent when he called on the Professor of Surgery, I. H. Cameron, to be told that this had been Mulock's choice, quite independent of any of the staff, including the Professor. The atmosphere was frigid, but a meeting with Mulock the next day restored warmth to the homecoming as the Vice-Chancellor explained that advice was sought from Dr. Adam Wright of the teaching staff, who remembered and recommended a native-born Canadian who had won the gold medal and a Fellowship.

CHAPTER 2

The Making of a Hospital

There was a bitterness in Bruce's voice when, in later years, he described his first experiences as Associate Professor of Surgery. His assignment was to teach bandaging to students for three hours a week and lasted for three years. He had not been made welcome, and time did not dull the sharpness of his reception. Of course, he was a surgeon, but there was little consideration for specialization at that time, as surgery was performed by anyone with a medical degree, and the fact that he was a Fellow of the Royal College did not carry much weight with those who were not Fellows. However, Peters appreciated his skills.

Cameron, who had vigorously opposed Bruce's appointment instead of his own nominee, Dr. Alexander Primrose, continued a cold relationship with the young post-graduate student, but the backing of Mulock was sufficient to ensure his re-appointment on a yearly basis.

Being in the Toronto General did not mean he was in the operating room. There were only 2 ORs and a large number of doctors had access, with the result that Bruce was forced to seek space in other sites. Fortunately he was able to make an excellent connection with St. Michael's Hospital, which had opened a few years earlier and welcomed the young man who was interested in doing brain surgery, and carried out several procedures that he had learned from

Horsley in England. One of these was the removal of an epileptogenic focus in the brain. This was causing an involuntary movement of the hand and arm, which had been described previously by Hughlings Jackson in the U.S. Bruce exposed the brain and identified the area that controlled the hand movement by stimulating various sites using a clay electrode. Having identified the focus, he removed that portion of the brain, an operation well in advance of any procedure that had been tried before in any part of Canada. Bruce reported that the patient's involuntary actions ceased.

He had always expressed an interest in concentrating on brain operations; however, he became more intrigued with working in the abdomen, particularly under the inspiration of Peters. It obviously was a stimulating change from bandaging. His practice grew rapidly, and in the first five years he was able to pay back the money he had borrowed for his postgraduate work. Since half of his patients were charity cases, it was necessary to balance the books by a sliding scale of fees for those who could afford the cost.

Bruce's office on Carlton St. was usually crowded and by 1910 he needed fifty beds in order to take care of his practice. Such a number would never be available at the General. There had been considerable discussion by the Board of Trustees as to the future of the hospital on Gerrard St., now growing older and handicapped by being far from the University. Joseph Flavelle (later Sir) and P. C. Larkin were members of a committee appointed by the University to investigate the possibilities of removing the General to College St., which eventually was approved, and funding was arranged from wealthy patrons of the hospital, who became honorary governors. These included Edmund Osler (later Sir).

The Board had always been the authority that gave permission for doctors to practise in the hospital, but with the organization of the new hospital, the University of Toronto took a much larger role. In truth, it had acted as a major stimulus for the upgrading. Because of the investment of money and the organizational skills of its Board of Governors and Senate, the University demanded, and received, a Joint Hospital Relations Committee. This committee would do all the hiring and the determination of privileges in the hospital. It decided that the hospital would not permit general practitioners — that is, it would be a consultant hospital. In 1907 the committee arranged that service would be provided in the hospital by three divisions of medicine and three of surgery. But this re-organization was not achieved easily. In May of 1908 the *Evening Telegram* printed that there was trouble ahead for The Board of Trustees of the General with its system of different services each with a responsible head. It reported that there was a bitter contest over the filling of the positions on the staff and "...for a time it was open warfare, for there were practically two camps, or rather only one camp, where the camp that did the campaign talking represented the younger element who claimed that older heads were not up-to-date, were behind the age in medicine and surgery, and that new blood was required on the Hospital staff."

Part of the problem was that there had not been a clear delineation of the responsibilities of the University and the hospital's Directors. While the University had entered into the arrangements with "wholeheartedness that evoked public appreciation," the hospital had not responded as fulsomely. It

agreed to appoint the three services but not to
appoint a special "University service" as demanded by
the University. Instead, the hospital stated, "We will
give Mr. Cameron the Professor of Surgery in the
University, five beds for each of the three services...
but no connection with the outpatient department."
But this appointment was a personal one, for
Cameron was not allowed to pass it on to the next in
line. The hospital Trustees stated that they were
responsible for the persons they appointed, and that
the University, although it had provided some money,
was not in the direct chain of responsibility. There
was dissatisfaction by some members of the hospital
staff concerning the people who had been chosen by
the University, and vice-versa. All of this intrigue and
confusion did not affect Bruce particularly, as he was
a University appointee, who was in charge of one of
the surgical services. This was indeed a long way
from his previous bandaging appointment. However,
although he had the position, he still lacked the
space, and this was limiting his income. The only
solution was to open his own hospital, which he was
able to do with the assistance of Mulock, Osler and
Dr. W. M. Caven.

The Wellesley was Bruce's bailiwick. It was conceived as a private undertaking, an institution
independent of University, government, or city officials. It gave him a perfect pitch for his practice,
which grew at a breathtaking pace. It provided a long
innings for him to perfect his skills at management
and personal relationships, and it was an ideal club
in which he could forge a team of social and business
contacts.

It was unusual for a private hospital to set up business in the city. While there were some special treatment centres for inebriates and mental patients, a

private general hospital for adults was unknown in Toronto. Of the public institutions, the Toronto General was the oldest and most prestigious. St. Michael's, which was operated by the Roman Catholic Church, had a special clientele. The Western, which had opened a few years previously, was still using tents, particularly during the milder months. Similarly, the Toronto Orthopedic Hospital at the corner of Bloor and Yonge streets, specializing in orthopedic problems, was also a tent hospital. Finally there was the Grace with its small bed complement. But The Wellesley, which offered an open door for Bruce's surgical patients, was unique. Of course, Bruce was sufficiently astute to permit any doctor to admit patients; however, the major surgical load was his.

His management skills were apparent even before the hospital was opened, when he purchased "Homewood", a private dwelling, in 1911 from The Honourable Lieutenant Colonel Frederic Nicholls. It was on Wellesley St. close to the corner of Sherbourne, and stood on four and a half acres of land. Bruce brazenly paid $65,000 for the property. He put down $20,000 and the remainder was a mortgage at 5 per cent. Then, through the auspices of his sponsor Mulock, Bruce caused to be formed a Board of Directors of The Wellesley Hospital Ltd. The name Wellesley was a result of stroking out "Homewood" and replacing it with a new name — which lasted into the next century. The corporation was headed by Miss Ethel Borrett, but the main force was Herbert A. Clarke, a partner in Mulock's firm. The first order of business was to purchase from Bruce the recently acquired property which he rolled over for the price he paid, taking back $20,000 in bonds instead of cash, permitting the hospital to be in business. The bonds were for $500 each and were scheduled to pay 5 per cent per annum. At the same time, Bruce bought 250 shares of the capital stock of the company for $25,000, and his associate Dr. William P. Caven took 50 shares, providing some working capital. So, by fronting the necessary cash to start the enterprise, Bruce had the protection of bonds and was willing to forego the interest he might have gained if he had left his money on deposit. The next 19 months were spent in building additions to Homewood in order to increase the available bed space. Bruce, who had been appointed treasurer of the Board, reported on January 13, 1913, that the building was almost finished but it had been necessary to admit patients in September of the previous year, due to the demand for beds. By December of 1912 he was able to show that the hospital was operating at 90 per cent capacity, with 346 patients having been admitted since September. He admitted that this had put considerable pressure on the rooms that had been set aside for nurses' accommodation, but this problem had been met by rental of temporary accommodation nearby.

In his report Bruce forecast that there would be an enjoyable profit in the future, particularly if the number of registered nurses employed could be reduced and replaced by student nurses. This bookkeeping was possible because the students did not receive any remuneration, although they did have room and board.

He announced in characteristic fashion that he had responded to the housing for the nurses problem by buying an adjoining house on Sherbourne St. from A. A. Allan, paying $25,500. He estimated, with appropriate alterations, would accommodate approximately 70 nurses and trainees in the future. He had put

down $5,500 and taken a mortgage at 5-1/2 per cent
for the remainder. His ability to handle his cash was
as skilful as his surgery. The action had been
approved by Mulock, without going to the Board of
Directors. It was not uncommon for Mulock to act in
such a manner.

Bruce then sold the Allan house to The Wellesley
for the purchase price and agreed to take back his
expenses plus cash payment for $9,766.40 in stock.
This meant that The Wellesley Hospital increased its
capacity without having to spend more capital,
except in anticipation of the interest and mortgage
payments, which might come due in the future.

Bruce's calculations were based on the projection
that income was anticipated well in excess of expenditures. The prospectus for the hospital read "Semi-
private patients would be charged $2.00 and $2.50 a
day and private patients would pay $3.00 and up."
This amount was in excess of what was charged at
the General, still located on Gerrard St. E. The
demand for admission was persistent and Bruce gave
a rosy picture of expected earnings, but by May of
1914, although revenue was still above expenses,
furniture and fittings were deteriorating and would
result in an overall debt. At that time negotiations
were begun with the Grace Hospital to consider a
merger. However, this union did not take place and
may have been a forerunner of several merger ven-
tures that were proposed over the next 80 years, in
order to staunch the flow of red ink.

Although the hospital was operating at close to
capacity, it was anticipated there would be increased
revenue if a greater number of doctors throughout
the province referred their patients. To this end a circular letter was addressed to Ontario M.D.s. Given
that The Grace Hospital merger collapsed, Bruce and

the Board felt it was advisable to seek help from the
province and proposed to change the charter of the
hospital to admit public, non-paying patients. This
was driven in part by the fact that the demand for
private beds during the war years dropped off and
more patients elected for semi-private. Consequently
the enthusiastic projections of profit did not material-
ize, and by 1916 it was recorded that 1,838 patients
had been seen below cost, and 348 at about cost, and
only 151 above cost. In 1917 the province finally
approved the change in the charter and non-paying
patients were admitted with the government paying a
standard daily rate.

All of these management problems were taken in
stride by Bruce but he did have expert assistance.
William Sykes, who was the accountant, maintained
a penny-pinching attitude as much as possible, to
prevent Bruce from unusual expenditures.

In Toronto, even with the war fever, there was
teaching and treatment to do and life had to proceed
as usual, especially as it was to be a short war. The
University course began in the fall and like many others, Bruce had extra work covering for those who had
left. The Wellesley continued to need direction and
especially, maintenance of the standards demanded
by a private hospital. The china was Limoges, the sil-
ver from Britain, the best possible beds and mat-
tresses, and the crest — a lion rampant holding a
pennant with the motto "Jamais sans Esperance" —
had to be emblazoned on the fine teapots and cream
jugs. The crest was adopted from the Wellington family, with permission. The slogan was adapted by
Bruce.

Even the most creative bookkeeping could not conceal an operating loss of $69,000 for 1913. Of course,
this was acceptable as it was laid down in the found-

ing documents that it was to be a non-profit institution. This loss was in part balanced by Bruce's gain as he found it an economic and efficient "...convenience to have all my patients under one roof."

A 1914 newspaper article acknowledged the deficit and justified it by stating that The Wellesley was not a "...resort for the wealthy... is probably the cheapest place in Toronto where an illness can be enjoyed with the exception, of course, of the public wards or charitable institutions. For $16.50 a week a patient can have accommodation in a semi-private room and for $25 a week, absolute privacy is secured." It was a popular hospital and occupied in great part by Bruce's patients, although contrary to other hospitals, any doctor could admit.

There was a dedicated staff, with Elsie Flaws — Elizabeth G. Flaws — as head nurse. She had graduated from the Toronto General School of Nursing in 1895 and subsequent to that had held several supervisory posts including a recent stint in Grand Rapids, Michigan. Bruce knew her from her time at the General and was able, after considerable letter writing, to persuade her to return to Toronto. She wrote, "It gives me a great deal of pleasure to accept the position of Superintendent of The Wellesley Hospital. It will be my ambition, to build up such a reputation for the nursing department that it will be on a par with that set by the physicians and surgeons. The hospital will simply have to be a success, if human effort can accomplish the desired result." Bruce had a particular talent for inspiring great loyalty from his hospital colleagues and with many other contacts — except possibly in the political field. Part of this flair may have been that he was never stinting in his praise for the efforts of others.

From the initial days, The Wellesley nurses had a

particular elan and were always considered as a social class superior to the General or the other hospital nurses. Some of this stemmed from the fact that many of the young women were from families who had received treatment at The Wellesley — indeed in some cases had been born in the institution. This particular identification with The Wellesley continued throughout its whole life and on occasion resulted in accusations of snobbery.

*   *   *   *   *

The elation at being recalled to Toronto, on the basis of his medal-winning examination performances, was deflated when Bruce ran headlong into the jealousies and pettiness of the medical faculty. This internecine feuding was intrinsic to a profession wherein ego and envy were bone and sinew of great clinicians who controlled by medical skill and political will. It had been and has been part of the ethos of medical education. However, once again, he stayed the course, operating in whatever hospital that would accept him and finally, after an emergency operation performed under frightening conditions on the son of William Mulock, he was able to convince a group of businessmen that a private hospital was necessary to care for his surgical patients. The Wellesley Hospital, although it provided Bruce with operating space, was never a financial success and passed from one cash crisis to the next. Eventually its volatile existence came to an end at the close of the century by government fiat. But Bruce was long gone by then, having survived many disappointments and storms.

CHAPTER 3

The Birth of a Medical Corps

There had always been a voluntary army, the Active Militia, which had proven its value on many occasions, but there had never been an organized medical service. The War of 1812–15 which the Militia saw as a great victory for themselves, discounting the fact that the British Regulars had been the major force, saw casualties being treated by local physicians and a few British Army surgeons. In 1866, during the Fenian invasion, 14,000 volunteers flocked to the colours. After the Battle of Ridgeway, the wounded were rescued by farm people in the vicinity, while awaiting the arrival of medical aid. In Toronto, when news was received of the battle, several physicians left by train arriving at Port Colbourne the following morning. Doctors J. Thorburne, J. Bovell, and W. Temple rushed to the battle area and were stunned to see the corpse of Temple's son, a medical student, who had volunteered to defend the country.

In 1870 Louis Riel led a rebellion at the Red River but there was little need for medical help. In a follow-up engagement in 1885, a group of physicians under Dr. James Bell were sent to the "front" including John Caven and his brother William Makepeace. Their major activity, as dressers, was to re-arrange medical stores and treat members of the 9th Quebec Voltigeurs. The unit was commanded by Surgeon-Major Campbell Douglas, who spent more time arguing with the Minister of Militia, Dr. A. B. Caron, than administering. The problem centred on getting adequate supplies and pay for the medical personnel. There was a stream of letters and telegrams, mostly demanding that the medical unit be placed on a proper footing, with funds. However, the Minister failed to come up with sufficient money, prompting an advice to him to apply to the U.S. for help on humanitarian grounds. Caron refused. He had other problems. Dr. G. T. Orton had sent a sizzling wire stating he did not think any man had the right to be his medical superior in the volunteer service and consequently he held Caron responsible for any deaths that occurred. Caron ignored that blast. This acrimonious relationship between field workers and headquarters staff formed a template for years to come.

About the same time a contingent of 378 Voltigeurs, raised and paid for by the Imperial Government, were active on the Nile under Surgeon-Major J. L. H. Neilson. The rivermen had been requested by General R. Wolseley who had used them in his rapid deployment to the Red in 1870. This contingent did not wear uniforms but was considered military, under the command of Lt. Col. Fred C. Denison. He had no love for the Imperial Military staff and on frequent occasions had criticized its actions in Canada. Neilson's experiences in this campaign, and his lack of friction with his superiors, merited his appointment to head the "Canadian Military Army Medical Department" in 1899.

The first real challenge to a re-named Canadian Army Medical Service (CAMS) was the Boer War, when out of a total of 749 Canadians, 65 died of wounds and 79 from diseases or accidents. These casualties resulted in a general order from the Canadian government for a re-organization of the entire army services along the structure of the War

Office in London. The directive stated that the "Director General of Medical Services shall be under the supervision of the General Officer Commanding and be charged with the administration of the Medical establishment." This was amended in 1904 when Minister of Militia Dr. Frederick Borden proposed a new set of army regulations which incorporated the CAMS. However his regulations were not the King's Regulations, the bible of the British services, but stated, "We shall rely in the future upon the regulations made in Canada, for the administration of the Militia of Canada." This action was taken because of Borden's deep suspicion of the Imperial staff and his ardent desire to have the Militia responsible for Canada's safety. The re-organization preceded the final withdrawal of Imperial forces from Canada in 1906, when the Canadian Militia became a regular standing army.

There had always been threats to Canadian sovereignty. Although the War of 1812 had been forgotten by most, there was still a consciousness that Canadian territory had been invaded by "Our neighbours." During the American Civil War there was apprehension on the part of British and Canadian leaders that the hordes of Americans, still under arms, might turn their attention northward. Fortunately, jawing prevailed over warring, but it became a principle in Ottawa that there should be a defence plan. Later, historians would speculate if this threat led to the founding of a United Canada.

Given the vast territory to be protected, a tactic was conceived by the Imperial staff to give resistance, until British troops arrived. Without the redcoats, survival would be impossible. On the withdrawal of British garrisons there was a new sense of urgency to have a "Canadian plan," and those responsibilities suited the emotional status of Our Lady of the Snows which was yearning for independence and straining to be mistress in her own kitchen.

The Militia was commanded by British officers who reported to the War Office in London via the Governor General, who relayed information to the Canadian Government. This galled the young Confederation which in 1898 declared the need for a "National Army." The key to this army was to be the voluntary Militia.

Colonel Edward T. Hutton, in command of all military matters, was impelled into this decision in 1895, just after the Jamieson raid in South Africa suggested an imminent conflict. Following this, the Venezuela crisis when the U.S. and Britain were on a collision course suggested, once again, that there was a threat to Canada. This was replaced by a standoff between the Yanks and Canucks when the Alaskan panhandle was disputed. Once again diplomacy prevented gunfire, but it was necessary for that "National Army" to send soldiers to back-up the RCNWMP.

The pace for military reform was heightened during the South African War. Canadian men on the street were heart and soul with any British cause, as most of them were expatriates, and when the conflict commenced, there was overwhelming public sentiment to send help. Prime Minister Laurier, reluctant to do so because of the cost, acknowledged the need for aid but not necessarily aid itself. However, his hand was forced when the Foreign Office in England gratefully acknowledged an offer from Canada to send two contingents. In truth this offer had no basis in any official communication. The Foreign Office made the action palatable by agreeing to pay part of the cost.

The Canadian force, which included several prominent Canadians, had a memorable transit on a steamer, The Sardinian, nicknamed the Sardine Tin, and finally arrived at the theatre, including one Canadian in mufti. He was Sam Hughes (later Sir).

Hughes was a swashbuckling Canadian version of a meld of Teddy Roosevelt and Winston Churchill. He had volunteered as a youth in the Fenian invasion and later took a three-month military course, and was appointed Lieutenant and finally Captain in the Militia in 1878. Early in his career he showed contempt for the "Red Tapism" of administration, preferring field soldiering. He became an expert rifle shot and formed the first drill squad at the Toronto Collegiate, which led to Cadet corps throughout the city. He was an outspoken proponent for the Militia and felt that a citizen soldiery based on the Swiss system was the preferred arrangement for Canada. Generally he was scornful of the Imperial Army system, with its chain of command and networks of communication, and he regularly outraged friends, foes, and superiors by ignoring those normal channels. But, in spite of his foibles, he was a close friend of Sir John A. Macdonald, and a voluble protagonist of the "national dream". John A. had remarked, "Sam Hughes is one of our best friends."

Because of his stern Methodist background, as a non-smoker and tee-totaller, he was able to allay a mother's worry, when he proposed that all good eighteen-year-old farmboys should join the Militia and be prepared to fight when the time came.

His keen advocacy of the citizen-soldier led to many clashes with regular army officers, who sneered at a military organization, which had been formed in 1868 and consisted of poorly organized battalions, commanded by under-trained officers. These sentiments, expressed orally and with body language by the Imperial-appointed General Officer Commanding (GOC) insured that funds for summer camp training took second place to regular army needs. Hughes reacted to this by gathering a group of supporters, including Dr. Fred Borden, a surgeon, Liberal and Minister of Militia, and kept up a drumfire of criticism of the excesses of GOCs. Hughes' ability to recruit non-Tories to his plans was a mark of his spellbinding abilities. As a hereditary Tory and Orangeman dedicated to the credo that "No Grit Dogans get Tory offices," he displayed remarkable persuasiveness.

Originally a school teacher, he purchased *The Warder* newspaper in Lindsay, Ontario; then he ran as a Tory candidate in 1890. His platform was the old flag, the old leader, the old policy and Sam Hughes. In spite of his singular vocal prowess, he was defeated, but made a remarkable recovery when election fraud was charged, winning the by-election. Even though they were on opposite sides of the house, he maintained excellent relations with Fred Borden. But Hughes could play both sides, and off the floor became an ardent supporter of Fred's cousin, Robert Borden, who became Tory leader.

While in government, Hughes never had any self-doubt that Canadians could do it better and he resisted all attempts by the GOC to reduce funds either for Militia training, or for the number of Militia units. His outspokenness, particularly when tinged with orangeism, branded him as a loose howitzer with a light lanyard and led to frequent recantations and apologies to the party.

In addition to political and journalistic skills he designed and patented a ventilating system for railway cars which won a prize at the Academy of Science in Paris.

As a self-promoter Hughes was eventually appointed Lieutenant Colonel in the Militia and embellished his standing by persuading Sir Donald Smith of the CPR to fund a trip to attend Queen Victoria's Diamond Jubilee in London in 1897. On the lawn at Windsor he rubbed shoulders and shook hands with Lord Roberts of Kandahar, Sir Redvers Buller, and Lord Wolseley of Ashanti. At the same time he was presented to Joseph Chamberlain of the Foreign Office and made sure that he kept addresses for future communications. Although to some his militia rank qualified him barely as a "sham warrior", on his return to Canada he was able to give an extra fillip to his brass and was sponsored by Smith to tour the British Australian territories as a travelling Empire evangelist, preaching the gospel of colonial military contributions for Imperial defence. Hughes' theme was built on "the British Bible and the British bayonet."

Six months before hostilities began in Africa, Hughes proposed to Prime Minister Laurier that a brigade should be developed for Imperial duty. This suggestion was not done solely on a basis of patriotism but more to demonstrate the amount of progress to self-independence that had been made in Canada. With the commencement of the war Hutton proposed to send 1,200 men to the Transvaal and that Hughes should be in command of a column. However Hughes, in response to Australia volunteering and paying for a brigade, stormed in the House that it was a national shame that Canada had been so miserly with payment, and offered to lead a force of volunteers himself. Fred Borden supported the concept of the Militia involvement. Hughes then wrote letters to Joseph Chamberlain with his plan, signing as Lieutenant Colonel, Commander of the 45th

Victoria Battalion. The letter was official military business that had not gone through the proper channels. Hutton reprimanded Hughes for going over his head and struck his name from the South African contingent. Hughes, characteristically, apologized, but Hutton was relentless and the solution to the impasse came only from Borden who approved Hughes accompanying the contingent, but as a civilian. Hughes, trading on the confusion that had resulted from mixed communications received in the F.O. was able to don his uniform on landing and was appointed as Supply and Transfer Officer, supporting Roberts. At the same time he struck up an acquaintance with *The Times* correspondent, Leo Amery, a rising journalist who later wrote a six-volume history of the war. Amery was full of scorn and criticism of the officers whom he charged with being responsible for more English deaths than the enemy. His anti-Imperialist articles found enthusiastic support from Hughes. Over the next several months Hughes distinguished himself with his audacity and ability to lead raiding parties. On at least two occasions he took prisoners by bluffing and on two other occasions he strongly criticized his commanding officer, making sure that his complaints were leaked to Amery. In a daring raid, he was able to occupy a position, although ordered by his CO not to do so. This resulted in a compounding of his criticism of Hutton and the local CO, leading Lord Minto, the Governor General of Canada, to cable Roberts telling him "to take steps to check this as the effect of any further publication is most detrimental to the position of any Imperial officer in authority." Roberts fired Hughes and sent him back to Canada "by the first ship."

By 1902 at the end of the war, it was obvious that the colonial volunteer soldiers had done their job well, frequently better than the British regulars. Hughes, repatriated early, remained an active veteran frequently advocating help for ex-servicemen and railing against the red tape of the regular army. In 1903 he was promoted to Brevet-Colonel and was also made unpaid Headquarters Railway Intelligence officer and appointed to the Board of Visitors of the Royal Military College in Kingston.

Although Hughes was re-elected in the next election, the Conservative party plummeted; even Robert Borden lost his seat. Hughes offered to step down but Borden refused and began a rebuilding process with the Provisional Central Committee of the party. Ominously, Hughes was not on the committee and instead Borden took H. M. Amies and George H. Perley from Quebec and A. E. Kemp from Ontario. All were wealthy and had solid social and business connections, and were "safe," compared to Hughes, who was still seen as a potential hazard, because of his bigotry towards Roman Catholics and the French. He was also concerned about loose immigration laws and charged that lawmakers favoured non-Anglo-Saxon Catholics over good British stock. On one occasion he described the arrival of immigrant French priests as a "curse to Canada."

As a champion rifle shot and President of the Dominion Rifle Association, he fraternized with millionaires such as Edmund Osler and James Gibson, the Lieutenant-Governor of Ontario. This brought him closer to Fred Borden, who had adopted a rifle design by Sir Charles Ross near the end of the Boer War. Borden encouraged the Liberal government to establish a factory to manufacture the Ross, as a new industry in Canada with tax rebates etc. in place of the British choice of the Lee-Enfield. Fred Borden included Hughes on his committee of procurement of the rifle, which was faster and more accurate, and solved the problems of chronic late deliveries from the British suppliers.

Hughes was re-elected in 1909 and once again was advocating the Ross rifle, particularly after the Canadians won the target-shooting contest at Bisley. However, the British National Rifle Association disqualified the victors on a minute technical point, which gave Hughes a fine opportunity to increase national pride against the Imperial authorities. But in his desire to win the contest Hughes had asked for a re-designing of the weapon so that the matching tolerance was tightened and it was transformed from a combat weapon to an excellent target firearm. Many Canadian soldiers died because the Ross rifle jammed during trench warfare.

Although Hughes continued to be outside the inner circle of the Conservative party, charging that his camp had "...more brains in five minutes than Perley or Amies have in a lifetime," the Conservatives won the 1911 election. It was necessary for Sam Hughes to give a weepy promise about future behaviour in order to have Robert Borden appoint him as Canada's Minister of Militia. Hughes promptly broke his word by criticizing Kemp and prophesying that a war would come with Germany and it might be necessary to launch a pre-emptive military strike.

When Professor Anton von Eiselberg hurriedly left the International Congress of Surgeons at London in June of 1914, Bruce immediately appreciated the gravity of events. Von Eiselberg of Vienna, a protegé of the great Billroth, rushed to board a German ship sent expressly to take him back to the continent. Bruce realized that the Declaration of War on August the 4th would alter his life, and lost no time in catching a steamer to Canada. Little did he know how great would be the transformation.

The Declaration, which was answered with a "Ready, aye, ready" from the colony, came in surprising sequences to Canadians, who had been led to believe that the British government was peace-minded. Not so to Sam Hughes, who recalled, to all who would listen, that he had predicted this war two years previously. He immediately began to recruit 25,000 men for the first contingent. Canada did have a war plan, drawn mostly for protecting its borders, but impetuously Hughes scrapped it overnight and launched a passionate call for volunteers to join local regiments, prior to assembling at Valcartier.

The original plan included a Director of Medical Services, Surgeon-General G. Carlton Jones, a veteran of the Boer War, who had been appointed by Prime Minister Laurier. Hughes, now Minister of Militia, up-dated the organization by forming, on paper, an Army Medical Corps with sixty-three medical officers and other ranks. Behind this group was a Medical Reserve Corps which had been established by Dr. J. Fotheringham of Toronto. Bruce had been appointed Lieutenant-Colonel, on Fotheringham's invitation and like many of his colleagues volunteered his services in the active force. George Nasmith, one of his students, was taken immediately to supervise the health and sanitation at Valcartier.

Over the next two months an army was assembled from all over Canada. Valcartier, the base camp, was built with frantic speed, including a rail connection to Quebec City and in short order Hughes was able to review the Canadian Expeditionary Force. It was a virtuoso performance, accomplished mainly by a sweating, bawling, exhorting Hughes who did it his way, rather than by the book which had been written by the professional soldiers over the preceding years. In spite of the lack of proper equipment; the need for a clear military organization; and the absence of training, the Minister of Militia, with suitable self-effacement, could announce on the departure of the CEF, "Men. The world regards you as a marvel."

Hughes was knighted for his effort.

* * * * *

The frenetic performance by Hughes resulted in the creation of a Canadian army, but there was little attention paid to building a complementary medical service. There were few committed surgeons in Canada, except for Bruce and others in university centres. A small number had experience with battle casualties. There had been little training of doctors to equip them to handle the diseases generated when large numbers of men were encamped. The experiences of the Boer War gave little knowledge of how to treat tetanus, trench fever, shock, or battle fatigue.

The military establishment had made some preparation for conflict, but the medical service had little except manuals from the Boer war, or even the Riel rebellion. Each of these was of little use for WW1.

CHAPTER 4

An Inquiry Is Conceived

Governments are immune to the cut and slash of parliamentary debate. While newspapers deplore, investigating committees decry, and voters demonstrate, most leaders can weather the storm. In wartime the echoes of jingoism and the platitudes of patriotism are sufficient to hold a steady course, even when the news from the front is bad. However, there is one lynch-pin which can unleash a flood of passions threatening any government with disaster. In spite of the defeats in the Crimean War it wasn't until Thomas Chenery, *The Times* correspondent, dispatched that "No sufficient medical preparation had been made for the proper care of the wounded," that John Bull demanded action. There was an immediate outpouring of help from private charities, but there was no resisting the roar for the recall of Lord Raglan, who was held responsible for the chaos in the hospital at Scutari. Death by shot was dulce et decorum; not so death in the shambles of an army hospital.

Similar disclosures of the carnage surrounding surgeons in the armies of both North and South in the American Civil War rocked government houses. The Boer War was a classic example of military intelligence failing to learn — in multiple areas. Given the incompetence in the field, it was even more devastating for readers of *The Times* to learn that "Men were dying like flies from want of adequate attention" and that the Army Medical Corps was not equipped for a war. With 22,000 dead, it came as a shock that 14,000 had succumbed to sickness and lack of medical attention.

To Hughes, who was under threat in 1916 from an investigating committee of the procurement of military stores, there was the ever-increasing load of Canadian casualties to threaten his future.

At the second battle of Ypres on April 22, 1915, Canadian troops peering over No-Man's-Land saw a green cloud creeping over the desolate mud. "That must be the poison gas that we heard big rumours about," said Captain George Nasmith to his assistant, Captain A. Rankin, as they observed the opalescent cloud expand, ascending here and there with brown puffs mixed into the general yellowish colour. By this time Nasmith's eyes were tearing and bloodshot, his throat and lungs rasping and hawking. A Canadian Highlander, face swathed in bandages, appeared. He reported that his platoon had been gassed, the Germans had surrounded them, and it was every man for himself. "Across the fields coming towards us, we saw men running, dropping flat on their faces, getting up and running again, dodging into disused trenches and keeping every possible bit of shelter between themselves and the enemy while they ran. As they got closer, we could see they were French Moroccan troops, and badly scared."[1] It was apparent that the Moroccans had given way and there was a break in the line. Within a few minutes Nasmith felt "pride of race" when up the road from Ypres came a platoon of Canadian soldiers to fill the gap.

It was serendipitous that Nasmith was in the field when the first chlorine gas was released. He had been appointed by Hughes to establish a sanitation unit and had already used the chemical to sterilize water, successfully maintaining the health at Valcartier without one case of typhoid. He had used the same methods in setting up portable water units on Salisbury Plain and now was doing similar work at the front.

On his return to No. 3 Field Ambulance, "lying on the floor were scores of soldiers with faces blue or ghastly green in colour, choking, vomiting, and gasping for air and their struggles with death, while a faint odour of chlorine hung about the place." Like many of his fellow officers, Nasmith was shocked, "at the nation which had planned in cold blood the use of such a foul method of warfare, should not be allowed to exist as a nation but should be taken and choked until it cried for mercy." In the casualty area he aided Captain Francis Scrimger, a graduate of McGill University, who had just returned from leave after being wounded and was awarded the Victoria Cross the following day, "...when he carried a severely wounded officer out of a stable in search for greater safety. When he was unable to carry this officer further he remained with him under fire until help could be obtained ...during the heavy fighting Captain Scrimger displayed continuously day and night, the greatest devotion to duty among the wounded at the Front... ."

There were others who were outraged at the use of gas. Captain R. J. Manion from Pembroke, Ontario, who had studied medicine at Toronto with Bruce as one of his lecturers, wrote in *A Surgeon in Arms* after his discharge, "...fighting with gas is cowardly and is against the rules of civilized warfare. Only a race which cares for naught but success, no matter how attained, would employ it." Warfare was still considered "civilized" by some.

The Canadians were rapid to develop methods to

protect themselves, urinating in a handkerchief and using it as a mask was sufficient to reduce some of the chlorine's effect. The French kept hay in a barrel in the trench along with bottles of sodium thiosulphate and when the alarm was given, soldiers dipped a handful of the hay and held it over their noses. By June 1915, British soldiers were issued with smoke helmets, with goggles, covering the entire head. Some units used a large gas pad tied with tapes around the neck and a strip for the eyes. Overall the gas devices were uncertain until the introduction of box respirators, which became standard in 1917. Horses, which were the backbone of the transport system, suffered severely, and all that could be done for them was to fit their nose bags with a thiosulphate preparation. Most died.

Bruce, disappointed that he was not chosen to go with the First Contingent, decided to go overseas as a volunteer. As he explained, he was unmarried. As a Lieutenant Colonel substantive in the militia on July 7, 1915 he wrote a letter to Sir Edmund Osler, asking him to use his influence with the Minister of Militia to send Bruce overseas, and offering to pay his own passage. Hughes supported the request and Brigadier General Carson wrote to Surgeon General G. Carleton Jones, Director of Medical Services (DMS), to "Make suitable arrangements because it had been strongly urged by friends in Canada." The DMS was not enthusiastic, being of the opinion that there were surgeons overseas of equal ability to Bruce. He reluctantly agreed that Bruce could be used as a surgeon in one of the hospitals, but did not feel that Bruce's services should be gratuitous, from a disciplinary standpoint. Further correspondence stated that Prime Minister Borden and the Minister had discussed the offer and the DMS was instructed to utilize Bruce's services in any way best suited to his ability.

On arriving, Bruce was greeted by the DMS with a curt statement that he was not required; however, he was then appointed to duty at the Duchess of Connaught, Canadian Red Cross Hospital, Taplow, England, on August 9. Undaunted by his frigid reception, and after observing the activities of the Taplow hospital, Bruce wrote to Jones to remind him of a desire to go to France at the earliest date. This precipitated a chain of letters between Jones, Carson, and Hughes and the proposition was accepted, once again grudgingly, on the basis that the experience would be of great value to Bruce to assist in the reorganization of the Medical Service after the war. Eventually the clearance came through and he was posted to the Number 2 Canadian Hospital at Le Treport, where he was greeted with a case of shrapnel close to the spinal column of a soldier. The CO and the staff did not feel that they had the competence to handle this, so Bruce removed the steel. The following morning he met Jones who, in spite of the operation performed the previous day, informed him that he had no need of a surgeon. Bruce accepted this decision and said he would return to Canada where a number of people were awaiting his services, but Jones barked "You stay here until your order papers come through!"[2]

But Bruce was not content away from the operating table and immediately repeated his request to proceed to the front. This caused another top-level conference between Carson, Hughes and Borden, and it was decided that the surgeon should not be treated differently from anyone else and no advantage was seen to the service in letting him proceed to the front merely as a spectator. Battleground tourism was looked upon with disfavour. Whether permission was given or not Bruce went ahead, in his Lieutenant Colonel uniform, to visit several areas.

Being satisfied with his tour, Bruce wrote to the DMS asking to be recalled from Le Treport, the Number 2 Canadian General Hospital, as he had promised to return to Canada on September 25, to resume his University teaching duties. Of course, the DMS did not agree, as he had not been apprised of this plan. This necessitated that Bruce ask Carson to telegraph the DMS that all was in order. While the administrative wheels remained frozen, Bruce took the matter into his own hand and tendered his resignation from the CAMC, in order to return to Toronto. Resignation was accepted on September 24, 1915, however there was still a problem in that Jones would not issue travel warrants. Bruce set off without them, pulled rank on the pier at Boulogne, bluffed his way past the assistant transportation officer, arrived in London where he wangled a ticket, together with the necessary documents on a CP boat sailing from Liverpool.

Once in Toronto, he hurried to the operating room and started on the waiting list of patients.

During his inspection of the front lines, Bruce had seen Nasmith in action and back in Canada he reported in *The Globe* on November 9, "Captain Nasmith, former Director of the Board of Health for Toronto, made the first report at British headquarters on the gas that was used when the Germans broke through at Langemark. His opinion has since proved to be correct and his recommendations, the best means for counteracting. His suggestion was immediately adopted by the War Office."

But even though means had been devised to mitigate the full impact of the gas attacks, casualties continued to increase.[3] On May 13, 1916, Borden reported there had been 22,000 casualties in the Canadian Forces. From the 290,000 who had enlisted in the first phase of the war, 247,000 were part of the fighting force, and 111,000 of those had gone overseas. In addition to the 22,000 there had been "wastage" of 21,700. This number of casualties was beginning to affect many Canadian households, and there were searching questions about the reason for such horrendous figures. In London, there were attacks on the RAMC in Parliament and Director General Arthur Sloggett was criticized for failures in the care of the wounded.

By July 1, 1916, the Battle of the Somme began and devastating news was received of terrible losses in the Newfoundland Regiment. The terrible toll continued and Hughes, who had been brooding for some time that there were serious problems with the medical services, had approached Bruce in the spring of 1916, to conduct an inquiry into the work of the Canadian Army Medical Corps overseas. Hughes knew of Bruce's voluntary service in the previous year and he had knowledge of the doctor's place in the Tory party and of his surgical skills through Edmund Osler. Mrs. Hughes had recovered successfully from an operation at The Wellesley the previous year. But most importantly Bruce had established a reputation of being outspoken and never tied by red tape.

It did not come as a surprise to Bruce when asked by the Minister of Militia to conduct an inquiry into the CAMC. Questions had been raised about the delay in bringing the Second Division, including the medical units, into action. While the problems of lack of organization which plagued the First Division could be overlooked because of the rapidity of the response from a country which was not prepared for war, surely by the time the Second set sail from Halifax on April 21, 1915, everything could have been top-drawer. But no, the Second Division was not in action until the fall because of chain-of-command problems and equipment deficiencies. Hughes, speaking in 1916 to the Empire Club in Toronto, blamed British obduracy for insisting on replacing Canadian-made supplies. And then too, there was the matter of Number 4 General Hospital, organized by the University of Toronto, having been posted to Salonika. There were no Canadian soldiers in that arena, so why send a much-needed unit to the Dardanelles?

It was fitting that Bruce, the second Canadian to be admitted to the Royal College of Surgeons, should examine the effectiveness of a service that was concerned with the casualties of war. During his FRCS training he had attended the clinics of the eminent brain surgeon Victor Horsley (later Sir). Sir Frederick Treves, who had saved the monarch's life with an appendectomy, had taught abdominal surgery, and Christopher Heath had demonstrated the principles of antiseptic surgery. Most of Bruce's teachers and peers were in the service and realized his talents. Although he had limited experience in the treatment of gas gangrene, which was the fate of many wounded soldiers, with resultant death or amputation, he was not convinced of the ultimate outcome of the reliance on germicides. This treatment, consisting of irrigating the wound with flavine, an aniline dye which had been shown to destroy bacteria in a laboratory, was used by many surgeons. Contrary to that, Dr. Henry Drysdale Dakin and Alexis Carrel of France combined efforts to develop a method of continuous irrigation of wounds with saline solutions, which controlled infection. From his own experiences, Bruce eventually became convinced of the efficacy of debriding the wound widely before using a germicide.

This was not an academic exercise as there was a major difference of thought and technique of treatment between the U.K. surgeons and the Canadians. The British, drawing on Boer War experience, still held that a projectile could traverse the belly without damage to hollow viscera. The number of amputations was rising. The American surgeon John B. Murphy taught Bruce and other Canadians that a septic knee joint should be controlled by the injection of an antiseptic, such as formalin. But the British inserted drainage tubes into the knee, before sending a casualty down the line. This protocol usually resulted in gangrene, followed by dismemberment. With the Murphy technique, the base hospital surgeon could open the knee, cut away damaged muscle and remove foreign bodies, then approximate the skin by loose stitches over a dressing without drainage, thus barring bacteria from marching up an open roadway. This delay in primary suture was a major surgical advance; and the wound was closed after four days if it looked and smelled clean. It was the same principle that was used in abdominal procedures. Bruce, a meticulous operator, rarely developed infections, and insisted on expert nursing care to avoid any complications.

In addition to his general abilities, Bruce had an enviable record of founding and administering The Wellesley. It had been no mean feat to create and build a hospital without government or institutional funding, to raise the capital, assemble the staff, and provide acclaimed care to a large number of patients. The province gave a grant to all other hospitals during the first ten years of existence at the rate of 20 cents per day. However The Wellesley, "For Private Patients Only", did not accept any government money, and quickly became known throughout southern Ontario. It was patronized by the wealthy and powerful, including the Mulocks, the Eatons, the Pellatts, and the Masseys. The Board of Directors was tycoon-heavy with Sir Edmund B. Osler, MP; Chief Justice Sir William Mulock, K.C.M.G.; Sir Martin Clarke, LL.D., K.C., previously Lieutenant-Governor of Ontario and the Honorary President was His Honor Colonel Sir John M. Gibson, K.C.M.G., Lieutenant-Governor.

This community of patients and politicians was the direct result of Bruce's skills, in and out of the operating theatre. Although other surgeons in Toronto, including C. L. Starr, Alexander Primrose, Frederick William Marlowe, F. N. G. Starr, and N. J. I. Yellowlees, used The Wellesley's OR facilities, it was Bruce who carried the major load with a daily list of at least four procedures.

In addition to a great number of appendectomies and gynecological repairs, he performed orthopedic surgery, including screw and plating for fractures. This technique had been pioneered by Sir R. Arbuthnot Lane in 1894 and upgraded by Henry Clapp Herman in 1912. Other procedures new to Toronto were neurosurgical repairs, alcohol injections into the fifth cranial nerve for tic douloureux, and the re-section of the spinal accessory nerve. During the early years of the war he removed shrapnel from several repatriated officers.

Bruce accepted Hughes' appointment, packed, and prepared to take up his important commission. However, there were two time bombs in his kit-bag. In his press interview on his return from France, he had stipulated that no dates or places be mentioned.

The reporter broke faith. This immediately prompted a thunderous letter from Lieutenant-General E. A. H. Alderson, GOC, Canadian Army Corps (France), to the Canadian High Commissioner in London, George Perley, including a newspaper cutting from the November 9th *The Globe*. The story mentioned the sector allotted to the Canadians after the severe fighting during the summer of 1915 in the second battle of Ypres, Festubert and Givenchy. The GOC claimed that this had been a very quiet sector, but after the newspaper article appeared, considerable strafing took place.

The second bombshell to explode was that Bruce, in his desire to gather teaching material for his lectures at the University, removed several X-ray plates of interesting fractures from the Le Treport. The films were missed, launching an immediate Army-style enquiry about how and why Bruce had removed them. The search eventually terminated just short of a charge of stealing army property. Everyone from Alderson down bristled and was anxious to prosecute. When Hughes heard of the matter, he snorted, "Just another example of red tape," and practically clapped Bruce on the back.

* * * * *

Bruce's visit to the war zone "at his own expense" was an unusual affair stage-managed by his political connections. He wanted to see with his own eyes how casualties were treated, and as he had not been called to service, he reasoned that going in the militia uniform, rather than a regular army outfit, would allow him to return to Toronto and his academic position. He was aware of the shortages of doctors on the home front. Although he enjoyed the perks of a uniform, he

*acted like a civilian outside of normal military conduct,
with regular officers who were denied coming and
going freely. His motivation may have been of the
highest level, but the outcome was a rock-bottom relationship with Jones, which set a level for the future.*

NOTES

1. Nasmith, G. G. *On the Fringe of the Great Fight.*
   McClelland, Goodchild & Stewart, 1917: 97.

2. Bruce, H. A. *Varied Operations,* Longmans, Green, 1958:
   89.

3. Manion, R. J. *A Surgeon in Arms.* McClelland, Goodchild &
   Stewart, 1918: 122.

   The Perley Papers, Archives of Ontario, contain the originals of other quotations.

CHAPTER 5

... and Aborted

On landing in England in early June, 1916, Bruce was vulnerable on two fronts. General Alderson, Perley, and Carleton Jones had not received an explanation of how he had taken French leave, crossed the channel, and then the ocean, without proper papers from his CO. Any other soldier would have been charged with desertion.

The second front explained the odd quiet on the first. Bruce — Hughes' boy — had been hand-picked from a number of equal or more qualified candidates. It was charged that many of them possessed what Bruce lacked — military experience, such as military know-how of a chain of command, filing reports, and military methods of handling casualties. Jones never relented from advising that there were other highly qualified officers available. But still, Hughes had picked Bruce.

This was not an unusual action by the Minister of Militia. Since the Declaration of war he had commissioned officers, dispatched them overseas — as supernumeraries, or on non-specific activities, or as plain and simple communicators — to act as his eyes and ears. His suspicion, amounting to paranoia, of the British High Command was justified, on many occasions, by its failure to pass on complete information. Hughes maintained that he was not told the truth or even part of it. His deep-down mistrust of the military establishment, for which there were ample reasons, could never be assuaged. In October of 1914 he had campaigned for Canada to have independent strategy and tactical control of the C.E.F. and to maintain its identity as Canada's fighting force. Perley, Major-General Sir William Gwatkin and Sir Eugene Fiset of Headquarter's staff objected and argued that Canadians should have the same status as regular British troops, and should be under the direction of the British government, which would administer, provide supplies, and look after the casualties. Perley proposed that Lord Kitchener, Secretary of State for War, implement a plan to have Canadian units broken up and trained with different regiments of Kitchener's army. It was not felt safe, by some, to use a purely Canadian unit at the front. Hughes swore that there was no way he would allow a British conspiracy to rob Canada of its identity and proclaimed to Kitchener that Canada had "...supreme control of the Corps." After all, Canada was footing the bill and raising the troops. This crossing of swords with Perley was a repeat of previous duels which had taken place over the past ten years and there had been no decrease of rancour. Perley appealed to Borden that Hughes was breaking out of normal channels and battling with the British command without a plan of action and to remedy this it was expedient for Perley to be given complete authority over Army administration in the U.K. Borden, although he realized Hughes' shortcomings, refused. The bombardment by Hughes of Perley and Kitchener's plan continued, and once again Perley demanded some relief from the disruptive actions of Hughes. Again Borden refused — but he mollified Perley by recommending that "Sir" be added before his name. It was a temporary respite.

Meanwhile, Hughes extended his personal network.

He appointed Lieutenant Colonel John Wallace
Carson (later Sir), a Montreal mining promoter, as a
personal representative and eventually chairman of
the Active Overseas Sub-Militia Council. Carson sent
news of events back to the Minister, which might not
have arrived otherwise. One of Carson's reports
described the deplorable conditions in which
Canadian troops were bivouacked on Salisbury Plain.
The report infuriated both Perley and Gwatkin. J. J.
Carrick, a land speculator, was given the rank and
job of official recorder. Major John Basset, publisher
of *The Montreal Gazette*, and Captain H. M. Daly were
commissioned as personal aides to Hughes.

Some of these appointments were transitory. Perley
managed to have Carrick withdrawn, but one major
coup by Hughes was securing Maxwell Aitken (later
Lord Beaverbrook). He became the Minister's inside
representative, looking out. Aitken, a Canadian and a
long-time Conservative, became the voice of the
colony in Britain. It was a loud voice as he published
the *Daily Express*, and was MP in the British
Parliament. He admired the dash and Kiplingesque-
type hurrah of Hughes and popularized him in a
book, *Canada in Flanders*.[1]

This band of appointees — Canadian national
extremists — sometimes worked easily with Perley
and others in the Canadian Headquarters staff, but
at other periods with difficulty as the degrees of xeno-
phobia rose with the perception of the ineptness of
the Imperial staff. All these scuffles took place in
front of a handful of the governing class of Britain
who watched the colonials with some amusement,
mixed with outrage. Hughes blamed Kitchener for the
reversals at Ypres and R. Borden complained that
Canadians received "...no more considerations than if
we were automata."

Aitken's appointment was of particular interest to Bruce as he was an old friend on the basis of being almost a patient. The New Brunswicker had an acute abdominal attack just before the war and started out to Toronto for an operation. Because of intense severity, he had an appendectomy in Montreal. Continuing to Toronto to convalesce, the two Tories met, through one of Bruce's nurses, and enjoyed each others company, becoming fast friends. When Bruce's son was born in 1920, he was christened Herbert Maxwell and Aitken was a godfather. The second godfather was Mulock, assuring young Herbert Maxwell entry to either political hall. Both godfathers were resolute, direct-action types, equally at home in a tea salon or a political brawl, and Bruce never failed to acknowledge his indebtedness to each. Aitken had broken into the financial world, guided by John F. Stairs, president of the Union Bank of Nova Scotia. Bruce enjoyed the story that Stairs sent Aitken off to "steal a bank," which he did in Windsor, Ontario, earning a $10,000 commission. The bank was absorbed into the Halifax operation. Following that, Aitken, by legerdemain, persuaded W. D. Mathews and Edmund Osler to surrender shares in the Hamilton Steel and Iron Co., with an enormous profit to Aitken.

In spite of the financial history, the victims and victor could be united in the doctrine of Imperial Preference and almost persuaded Aitken to run for Tory office in 1911. But Beaverbrook remembered the unhappy lot of Stairs, when he had served in both Federal and Provincial houses, and declined. Instead Aitken bought the Rolls Royce Company and sailed for England. He returned in company with Tim Daly, previous Governor General of South Ireland, to aid Hughes in his recruiting drive. Their ships almost passed each other as Bruce and Hughes sailed for

England in the summer of 1916. In Hughes' jacket was an order appointing the doctor as Inspector General of the CAMC. Following Hughes' approach to Bruce earlier in the year, Bruce had written several letters to the Minister urging that the appointment be announced; finally on July 20, 1916, the Minister signaled Carson that Lieutenant Colonel Bruce was appointed with the power and authority to inquire and report upon surgery and medical services generally of the Canadian Expeditionary Force overseas, and was to be appointed Colonel.

On arrival in England, prior to the official announcement, Bruce travelled around the country, meeting old friends including Sir William Osler. Their contacts had dated back to undergraduate and graduate years. Llewellyn Barker, Bruce's boyhood friend from Port Perry, had graduated from medicine in Toronto in 1889 and went on to Johns Hopkins for further training, in company with another Toronto graduate, Thomas Cullen. Barker succeeded Osler when the latter left for Oxford. Osler had maintained many connections with Toronto and was a frequent lecturer, especially at festive occasions, such as the opening of the U of T Biology building, when he spoke on malaria. Another lecture, which Bruce remembered and honoured was in 1903 at the opening of the new Medical Building, when the oft-quoted paper, "The Master Word in Medicine is Work." Of course a call to Osler's home in Oxford at 10 Norham Gardens was made, with visits to the Radcliffe and other hospitals; later he visited Cherkley, the Beaverbrook home.

This time was not spent just socializing. Observations were made and thoughts organized for the work ahead. The voyage across the ocean with Hughes laid out much of the ground work of what was expected. The basic premise was that Canadians should direct the Canadian armies and, although Imperials could advise, the chain of command was to be from the Minister of Militia to his appointees. Part of this credo was that Canadian casualties were to be cared for in Canadian hospitals, staffed with Canadian professionals.

It was not an unreasonable suggestion since in June of 1915 Colonel Hodgetts, Commissioner of the Canadian Red Cross, which was responsible for some of the wounded at the Queen's Canadian Hospital at Beachborough Park, had written a letter to Jones requesting a similar arrangement at other hospitals, for example the Duchess of Connaught Hospital, Cliveden. Jones agreed and gave instructions that the Canadian casualties should be directed to those centres. However this order was amended, after the British protested, and Jones diluted the order: "...it is not now considered necessary from a Canadian point of view, to make any special arrangements at Southampton for the collection of Canadian patients."

The committee for the Inquiry had been suggested by Bruce, and appointed by Hughes. It included Colonel Wallace Scott, Commanding Officer, Moore Barracks Hospital; Colonel Walter McKeown, Surgeon; Lieutenant Colonel F. W. E. Wilson, of the Canadian Training Division, Shorncliffe; Lieutenant Colonel Charles Hunter, a prominent Winnipeg physician; and Colonel Frank Reid, Director of Recruiting and Organization for the Canadian Expeditionary Force. Each of these appointees, except Reid, was an outstanding medical professional. Wilson had supplied a report to Ottawa the previous month in which he wrote that of 235 men who had arrived in a draft,

19 per cent were unfit. Reid had extensive records on the results of recruitment.

The committee members spread out over the country, visiting hospitals and treatment facilities. Bruce, in addition to directing, conducted an inspection of installations in France. While Carson had given instructions that the committee should receive full cooperation, there was hesitancy on the part of some field staff in France. A series of letters between senior members pointed out that Bruce had been appointed Colonel although he had limited military experience, only one month and seventeen days in the service overseas. Another communicator to Carson suggested disapproval of the methods Bruce used for gathering information. Underneath these comments was a strong feeling that a person with so little actual military experience other than a short hitch, should not be placed in full charge of such a large and important service. Even the matter of visiting any posts on the continent raised objections, and a letter from the War Office to Carson on August 21 pointed out that the appointment and the necessity of the visit was not understood, and that the authority could not be granted pending particulars. This was followed by a letter on September 5 advising that permission had been given for Bruce to go to France, providing it was understood that "...the mode of supervision of Canadian medical units with the army in France cannot be separated from normal control of all units throughout the Army and that the work of Canadian Medical units is not to be confined to Canadian troops only. Colonel Bruce will be accompanied by administrative medical officers of our bases."

Bruce maintained that the motive of the inquiry was to ascertain if everything possible, concerning medical and surgical skill and nursing, had been and was being done for the brave men who had been wounded or had become sick. This could be rendered only if the best service was available to the soldiers. A codicil to this was an examination of the method of administration of the Medical Services, which gained optimum results with the least waste of public money. He was aware, and took into consideration, the fact that at the beginning of the conflict the Medical Service was comparatively small and not pre-pared to cope with the large problems associated with a rapidly increasing force. This was not unique to the CAMC but applied across the board as far as the Canadian Army was concerned, which explained many irregularities which could be turned up by any investigator.

While such aberrations from normal procedures could be accepted by one person, another, depending upon his basic philosophy, would see gross errors.

It did not take long for Bruce to question why Jones had sent three hospital units to the Dardanelles via Cairo, when there were no Canadian troops in that area. Even though Jones had responded to an urgent request from the Imperial staff, it gave the investigating committee a good bone on which to chew.

A more immediate concern was that Jones had approved the setting up of a convalescent home for officers by Perkins Bull. He was another larger-than-life Canadian lawyer who had amassed a fortune through land sales and the war demand for Cuban sugar. He had contact with Hughes previously acting as one of the directors of a land-selling operation in western Canada. Having acquired funds, he settled in London. When the war broke out he was concerned with the number of Canadian officers who were convalescing but had no "home." Therefore he began to take selected ones into his house on Putney Heath where he provided stimulating conversation, and his wife made sure that tea was served. This voluntary action was given official imprimatur by Jones who recommended that Bull should receive a stipend per day for each officer. Mrs. Bull became enthusiastic about the activity and, since the house of Sir Ernest Shackleton facing her home was vacant, arranged to rent it and set up a convalescent hospital on a more formal basis. This involved using Voluntary Aid nurses. In addition the CAMC provided a car and driver and several NCO's for duty.

Although Bull had started this operation on the basis of meeting Canadian officers in Mayfair, the Administrative Officer of the Medical Corps now began to direct convalescents to the Home.

Bruce's committee found that despite the fact that the Home had been visited by the King and Queen and that Robert Borden was an honorary director, there was little administration or surveillance of the organization. Officers came and went as they pleased, there was no record kept of their stay, no medical supervision, and it appeared to be operating as a hotel rather than a convalescent home.

However, Bull continued to receive a daily stipend per occupant which, over the course of several months, amounted to considerable sums. On the recommendation of Captain J. Ewing for the DDMS to Bruce, it was suggested that this arrangement should be terminated and the car and driver and staff should return to normal duties.

On June 1, 1916, the Third Division CEF was routed from Mount Sorel with terrible casualties, including the commanding officer, M. G. Mercer killed and a Brigadier captured. Two weeks later the

Canadians stormed back to retake the hill, with 8,000 casualties. July 1 was the beginning of the Battle of the Somme when 21,000 soldiers in Kitchener's Army lay dead by nightfall.

Although the committee was frank and open to all in its mission, the usual reaction of defensiveness, which happens when any administrative structure is subjected to an investigation by an outside authority, was noted.

This foot dragging was inevitable when it was common mess talk that the chief investigator was not "regular" army and was reported to have no knowledge of "the army way." One other fusillade of friendly fire came from Sir William Osler. In August he sent a postcard to Bruce, saying, "Do come down one day soon, I wish to talk to you about the Commission. If it has an animus towards Jones there would be a row. The profession will not stand for it, and the composition looks suspicious. Here Tuesday and Wednesday."

Osler was well apprised of on-going matters in the CAMC as he was consultant to the military hospitals in England and had a special interest in the Duchess of Connaught Hospital at Taplow. It was not an unusual invitation, for Bruce had visited Osler previously and actually had received a visit from him when recovering from appendicitis in Toronto. At that time Osler had confided that he had been offered the post of Regius Professor of Medicine at Oxford but he would receive only £100 a year. In answer to Bruce's laughing statement that that would not be enough to live on, Osler pointed out that he invested any surplus earnings with his brother Edmund, from which he received a good income.

Bruce replied to the card, apologizing that he was

unable to come as he was off to France. As to his appointment he added:

> ...from the tone of your communication you are evidently labouring under a mis-apprehension as to the work of the Committee appointed in connection with the CAMC. For your information I may say that I accepted a commission from the Honourable the Minister of Militia of Canada to make an inspection of all hospitals and institutions to which the Canadian government is contributing and to report upon the conditions found, together with any recommendations for the improvement of this service... I have undertaken this work with the sole object of making an impartial inquiry into the organization and administration of the C.A.M.C. and without animus to anyone.
>
> If I had received a communication from anybody but yourself of this kind, Sir William, I would have looked upon it as a threat and considered it improper under the circumstances, but having had for many years the greatest admiration and the kindest feeling and affection for you, I'm quite sure you did not mean it at all in this way.
>
> On my return from France, at the end of another ten days or so, I shall be delighted to run up some day and see you.

Osler responded with a do come when he could. He then put on paper of his concerns regarding the composition of the committee: "To appoint men who are under Jones to report on the work of the Department, of which they are units seems unfair. Was Jones consulted as to the personnel of the committee?"

Bruce showed the letter to Hughes who suggested

that he should withhold any comment. However, Osler, wrote again on September 6 requesting an answer to his questions. By now Bruce was standing on his rank and replied:

> Must ask you, if further information desired beyond that contained in my letter, to kindly communicate direct with the Minister of Militia, Savoy Hotel.

Osler accepted this and answered that he had wired Hughes.

All was quiet on that front, temporarily.

The committee finished the report and the printers worked night and day to complete the production in order that Hughes could take it with him on his return to Canada. All members of the committee agreed with the 23 major criticisms of the Medical Services, and 14 recommendations which were made. It was labelled:

CONFIDENTIAL
FOR OFFICIAL USE ONLY

and given to Hughes.

The report included many meticulous investigations in the typical Bruce manner, and also some sweeping statements, which were overblown in some cases, in the typical Bruce manner. The main recommendation was that the Medical Services should be re-organized from "top to bottom," and a scheme was attached which urged that it should be adopted as soon as possible.

Drawing on the information that was gathered from Reid and others, a vigorous statement was made of the large number of soldiers who were arriving in England from Canada who were medically unfit and should never have been enlisted. This included not only underweight, under-age, or over-age, but also men with active tuberculosis, paralysis, or orthopedic disabilities.

A strong counsel was that instead of dispersing Canadian casualties over the entire U.K. from Northern Scotland to Ireland and Wales, steps should be taken for the collection of Canadian casualties at bases in France, so that they could be directed to Canadian hospitals in England. These hospitals should be concentrated in one area and the use of British hospitals for Canadian patients should be discontinued, if possible. This scattering of hospitals over a wide area was objectionable not only from the level of expense but also from the inability of medical officers to track the progress of the casualty and terminate care. Part of this concern was that there had been findings that there were unnecessary detentions in hospitals because of lack of supervision, which was blamed on the dispersion of casualties.

Contingent to this was a brisk proposal that Voluntary Aid Hospitals were inefficient, expensive, and unsatisfactory. Of course, this applied to the administration of the hospital and not to the staff, whether VAD, workers, or service personnel. The committee was careful to emphasize that the VAD women were excellent but required more training. The medical care in most VAD hospitals was given by civilian doctors who had received no army training and therefore were not in a situation where they could treat the patient effectively, or, more importantly, record the problems with a view to pensionability. In fact, Bruce was a strong supporter of the VAD nurses and proposed that a parallel organization should be set up in Canada.

There were 57 VAD hospitals around the Shorncliffe area and the committee felt that these were difficult to supervise, expensive to operate, and sometimes caused costly and disastrous mistakes. Mal-administration of hospitals was a frequent finding in the survey. For example, Red Cross hospitals were inefficient and were under dual control from the Red Cross and also from the Canadian Medical Service.

Supervision was a major concern at most institutions. The committee found that there were no guidelines laid down for the type of operations that were permitted locally and, alternatively, those which should be done in Canada. In the latter class those soldiers who would not improve their military efficiency, as the result of an operation, should be returned to Canada as early as possible. This recommendation, that serious problems such as nerve lesions, contractures, shell-shock, neurasthenia, and amputation cases should be returned to Canada for treatment, was reiterated for several hospitals. Currently there was insufficient facility to fit amputees with artificial limbs in England. There were also criticisms of the establishment of hospitals such as the one at Buxton, which was for the treatment of rheumatics, who should be repatriated.

A major advice was the care of Canadian venereal disease patients. Currently they were not in one special unit, and occupied beds more urgently required by other casualties. The committee argued that if these patients were kept at a high level of fitness, they could be returned to their fighting units at an earlier date.

Other matters such as promotions and dissatisfaction of medical staff were also recognized. In an overwhelming number of cases it was realized that the award of pensionable disabilities would be very difficult in view of the fact that Canadian doctors did not

have active surveillance of casualties, and the necessary records would not be available to pension
boards on the soldier's return to Canada.

In keeping with the general philosophy of Hughes,
and other Canadians, there was a strong criticism of
the fact that Canadian hospital units had been sent
to Salonika and Cairo when beds were needed in
England. Similarly, an investigation of a Canadian
hospital unit that had been sent to Paris, and sat for
several months without any patients, was noted.

In short, the report was a bombshell. It was presented on October 6 to the Sub-Militia Council,
whose members were Carson, Major General S. P.
Steele, CO of the Second Division, and eight other
high-ranking members of the Medical Service. It
included supporting letters from non-committee
members such as Lieutenant Colonel G. S. Rennie
who stated that if the recommendations were acted
upon, it would "...help greatly to improve the
Canadian Medical Service as a whole."

The Council agreed with the majority of the recommendations and moved that those contained in the
report should be put into effect under the administration of someone in complete accord therewith;
"...the Council recommends that Surgeon General
Jones proceed to Canada with a view to co-ordinating
these services, and that Colonel Bruce be appointed
Acting Director of Medical Services, C.E.F." The proceedings were forwarded to Hughes who replied with
instructions to give the necessary authority to Bruce
to proceed with the re-organization as recommended.

Bruce, however, replied that he did not want to be
Acting Director of Medical Services and suggested
that Colonel Murray MacLaren take that job.
MacLaren, a country practitioner, had been President
of the CMA in 1913, and then CO of No. I Canadian

Hospital at Étaples. In the thirties he became Minister of Pensions and National Health. Bruce preferred the scalpel to the pen.

Armed with the backing of the committee and the go-ahead of the Minister, Bruce initiated several changes. Orders were issued to physicians examining volunteers for much more stringent medicals, and a further examination to be made before permitting men to embark for England.

Bruce had detected a problem where No. 6 General Hospital was idle in Paris because it had no facilities and had been awaiting the erection of a hospital over the past five months. This was solved by persuading the French military authorities to provide a building at Troyes.

Instructions were drawn up to set a standard of medical fitness which applied to France, England, and Canada, and would insure that men would not be evacuated from the front on the basis of an individual medical officer's opinion. This was associated with a training period for medical officers.

Directives were made that if medical treatment was not to reach a stage of finality in less than three months, the casualty should be returned to Canada.

Arrangements were made for the transferring of the fifty-seven VAD hospitals around Dover to the direction of the CAMC, thereby saving Canada some $160,000 per year as the British authorities would no longer be doing the administration. This re-organization was stopped by the newly appointed Minister before it was completed.

On November 1, 1916, Perley was appointed to be Director of Medical Services in London by Sir Robert Borden, who was concerned that Hughes was once again on a rampage. Hughes had continued to make anti-Imperialist speeches and was causing considerable antipathy. His appointment of the Acting Sub-Militia Council in September, without consultation with the Prime Minister or Cabinet, caused even more problems as it was realized that this was a move to further the Minister's desires to direct the Army from his office. Perley, who had previously been Chairman of the Overseas Military Committee, was very disturbed over this unilateral action by Hughes and complained to Borden that it was just another instance of unforgivable actions by a "...conceited lunatic."

In spite of the victory that Bruce had gained in having his report accepted and recommended, he felt enfiladed. Perley, with obvious support from Borden, was blocking the re-organization. Bruce was also receiving fire from Lady Edith Drummond, the daughter of the Earl of Perth, a major figure in the British Red Cross and an important supporter of the VAD. She had a close friendship with Lady Astor and others who supported VAD hospitals, including General Arthur Slogget. Having read of Hughes' attack on November 9 in a speech at the Empire Club in Toronto, when he made charges against British Army administration and stated that "...thousands of Canadians had lost months and sometimes a year in hospitals not under Canadian control... and that Canadian soldiers were allowed to go under the knife of first year medical men while the services of experienced surgeons in Canada were not being utilized," she wrote a strong letter to *The Times* about Canadians taking over the VAD hospitals and implied that Bruce was criticizing the VAD workers. Bruce had been scrupulous not to do so, and although he realized that their training usually lasted only one month, he felt they did contribute but could not be considered nurses under any circumstances. His major suggestions with regard to the VAD hospitals, therefore, was not only that the Canadians should take over to save money, but secondarily to bring in a higher level of nursing.

Much more significantly, Lady Drummond felt strongly that a Canadian soldier should not be segregated from other nationals and in particular from the British. She was re-inforced by Lady Perley.

A third burst of fire was received from Osler. In a letter dated October 15 to Bruce, he expostulated that he had cabled his protest to Borden but had not received any satisfaction as yet. "I cannot tell you, Bruce, how sorry I am that a good man like yourself should have got mixed up in this affair ...so sorry for you!" However the major part of this letter was concerned with Taplow. The Committee of Inquiry had found that there was a major problem with the administration of the hospital as the Quartermaster, and possibly other members of the staff, were involved in a scam in which they sold Red Cross clothing, knitted in Canada, to civilians in the area. The affair surfaced when a Canadian knitter enclosed a note to a presumptive soldier recipient. The civilian who bought the clothing promptly reported this to the authorities and an inquiry was launched. Osler was concerned with what had happened to Miss "X". "I write to protest against the injustice done to Miss "X" and removing her at the same time with "N" and the QT. Master. I understand that the charges against them were for peculation, and removing her with them implicates her directly and puts a cruel stain on her character... could I see the findings of the committee? As a consultant to the hospital, and actively interested in it from the start, I think it is not unreasonable to ask for this."

Bruce explained that the committee of officers consisting of Reid, Colonel A. D. Macrae, Major M. Alexander and the Deputy Judge Advocate General had examined officers at the hospital under oath and after a very exhaustive inquiry, certain recommendations were made. The President of the Board and Jones agreed that Miss "X" should be removed. Bruce understood that she received another position as matron and "I am quite sure there would be no stain upon her character."

He then refused Osler's request for a copy of the findings which had been sent to the Sub-Militia Council, as he did not have them and as they had not been part of the Inquiry.

However, the letter went a little further. He picked up on Osler's comment:

> You are sorry for me. I do not quite know what you mean. I undertook a certain duty for the Canadian government at a considerable sacrifice, but only after careful thought. I fully realize that to make an inspection of a critical character into the Canadian Medical Service, would necessitate my disregarding entirely the personal element, searching in an unbiased way for the real conditions. It was quite apparent to me at the outset that in doing so I would incur the enmity of many interested persons, but as the good of the whole Medical Services and the welfare of the Canadian soldiers were of much more importance in personal considerations, I undertook the difficult task... This report, and a reply to it by General Jones, had been carefully considered and my recommendations had been approved and adopted by the Sub-Militia Council. ...for the work I've done and the position I have assumed, I have no apology to make. I think, moreover, as we will all be judged by our work, after a few months time, I

have no fear what the verdict will be. I may say in conclusion, that I regret very much that you felt called upon to take the attitude which you did from the beginning and which I consider, under the circumstances, entirely uncalled for and improper. I had only got nicely started in my work when I received a letter from you threatening me with certain consequences if it was continued in a certain way. I am exceedingly sorry to have to write you thus, but I do it with the kindliest feelings and warm personal regards.

By this time Osler had resigned as consultant in protest at the way the Inquiry had been handled, without Jones being involved in the selection of the committee. His resignation was published in the *British Medical Journal.*

Another missile impacted on November 11th. Borden asked for and received Hughes' resignation. This, of course, removed Bruce's friend at court, as was seen the following week, when Perley gave instructions to the Acting Adjutant General for Canada to arrange a Court of Inquiry "to which shall be referred the report on the Canadian Army Medical Services by Colonel Bruce and the interim report of Surgeon General Jones and as to whether the Bruce criticism was justified in whole and part and whether the recommendations by Bruce should be endorsed or not."

Perley had asked Osler if he would sit as President of the Court but was refused and instead chose, on the advice of the Imperial Staff, Surgeon General Sir William Babtie, K.C. M.G., C.B., V.C.; Colonel E. C. Ashton; Colonel J. T. Fotheringham; Colonel A. A. Ross; and Lieutenant Colonel J. M. Elder.

Bruce, who had been stunned by the publication of

his report which had been given to Hughes with a specific note that it was secret and confidential, was now choleric that a committee had been struck by Perley to investigate a report which had been approved by the Council consisting of five generals and five colonels. He also objected to the selection of the members of the Perley Court of Inquiry as three of the four members had no direct knowledge of conditions in England and had been on duty at the front in France. "It would appear that the Minister intends to white-wash effectively my report instead of facing issues," he wrote.

But the major objection was the choice of the President, an Imperial General, who was going to decide on the fate of Canadian soldiers. Despite Hughes' protests, Borden, who shared similar aspirations for Canadian autonomy, inconceivably went along with Perley's recommendations.

Within a week Bruce had another strong objection, this time about Fotheringham. Bruce had found out that he had issued statements in a Memorandum that strongly supported the appointment of Babtie and at the same time denigrated the Bruce report by stating that all was well with the Medical Services: "No occasion has arisen for any lack of confidence in the policy of the D.M.S in London." Bruce was outraged and asked Borden to be relieved of his position so that he could return to Canada, however he received no acknowledgement. He then took another tack and urged Perley to broaden the scope of the Inquiry and examine what was going on in the Medical Services by direct visitation and examination rather than looking at reports, etc. There followed a cat-and-mouse game between Perley and Bruce; letters and cable-grams exchanged almost on a daily basis with Bruce continually striving for his goal — a thorough investigation of the Medical Services — and Perley digging in to maintain the original terms of reference for the Court.

Interestingly Reid wrote a letter to Perley pointing out that although a Court of Inquiry had been appointed, it somehow had been transformed into a Board. This was a subtle difference because under Army Regulations a Court of Inquiry permitted the person "accused" of defence, being present over the whole hearing, of being able to cross-examine (through proper counsel). However the Board, only permitted Bruce to make a statement, and would not accept any other evidence from him, nor permit any cross-questioning.

Meanwhile in Canada the cause célèbre had been picked up. Questions were raised in the House, and editorials in *The Globe* asking that there be a full disclosure of all of the facts. But Borden, who was facing an election in the near future and therefore wanted to keep a cap on the issue, and refused to be drawn into an open argument with Bruce.

The *BMJ*, in an editorial comment, presumed that the Babtie Board would be able to sort matters out and implied that the Bruce Report would be shown to be hyperbolic. In opposition to this, forces in Canada came to Bruce's defence. Hector Charlesworth of *Saturday Night* printed several articles stating that Bruce's Report was what was needed for the Medical Services. The magazine also disclosed that Babtie was under investigation for a medical catastrophe involving British troops returning from Khut, Mesopatamia. These soldiers, a section of the Indian Army, for which Babtie was the Chief Medical Officer, had suffered severely because of lack of supplies and transport during their retreat. The debacle had been reported in the press, which led to a Parliamentary investigation of Babtie's role. Eventually he was cleared on the basis that he had left the Indian Service shortly before the event occurred. However *Saturday Night* neglected to mention this exoneration.

Osler, impervious to the previous comments made by Bruce, suggested in a letter on December 10th that all correspondence to Generals Hughes and Jones with regard to Taplow should be published, and asked Bruce to arrange for this. Bruce replied that he did not have the letters and could not possibly be responsible. Osler answered on the 21st, locating the letters and once again asked if Miss Campbell's name could be left out of the reports. She happened to be the daughter of one of Osler's old professors.

This letter came on the same day that the Babtie committee made its report. Shortly after that Bruce replied to Osler that he could not possibly publish the letters as they were not in his possession and suggested that Osler should contact Jones.

The Babtie Report was the ideal government exercise. It was all things to all people.

Bruce claimed that it was a vindication of the recommendations that his committee had made in advising that the Medical Service should be re-organized from top to bottom. While agreeing that the separation of Canadian casualties from British casualties was desirable, the Board advised it was "...impractical and impossible to do so." The Board felt the principle points emerging from the Bruce Report were the concentration of Canadian sick; the suitability of VAD hospitals and the system of medical boards." While admitting that the distribution of Canadian casualties was a complicated matter, the Board did not address the marked aberrations brought out by Bruce where, for example, two Canadians had been sent to a remote district in Scotland, a hundred miles from the central hospital, and could not be visited, owing to the two-day trip involved.

With regard to the claim that there was unnecessary detention in hospitals, the Board agreed that there was a considerable accumulation of convalescent patients in Imperial hospitals, but it blamed this on the inadequacy of Canadian facilities. It recommended that more should be provided in Canada.

The Board did not agree with Bruce's recommendation that the use of VAD hospitals should be discontinued. It countered the arguments of inconvenient location and difficulty in supervision and also added that there was adequate nursing staff. It took notice of the widespread resentment that had been generated by Bruce's comments and chose, as did Lady Drummond, to target these comments on the VAD personnel rather than the VAD administration.

Bruce's claim that Shorncliffe was operating inefficiently and was a tremendous expense to the Canadian government was discounted by the Board, which disagreed that the employment of the CAMC personnel would be more cost effective. The same argument was used with regard to CAMC personnel who were in the Imperial service, for example in Canadian hospitals, being located where there were no Canadian troops. The essence of this argument was that the Canadian Army was part of the British Army and it would be impossible to regard it as a separate entity. However the Board did not take cognizance of the Bruce argument that the priority should be given to Canadian casualties, without restriction of British personnel, space being available.

There was agreement by the Board and Bruce that

many surgical operations were being performed which would not increase military efficiency. Other criticisms of the Jones administration were softened because of lack of personnel, lack of facilities, both in Britain and Canada, and the general state of the CMAC organization which Jones had inherited.

In short, Bruce claimed that eleven of his fourteen recommendations had been agreed to or were in the process of being changed when the Board met.

Jones felt vindicated that many of the charges were known to himself and were in the process of correction.

The *BMJ* was relieved that its speculation of an earlier date had proven to be correct, and there was no possibility that Bruce would continue to make threats of litigation.

Borden was mollified that the situation had been defused and would no longer be a time-bomb in the forthcoming election.

The professional soldiers were happy that this pushy type had been put in his place.

Lady Drummond was satisfied that her argument against "segregation" of Canadian troops, a term which she had introduced in her original letters to *The Times*, was justified.

Perley was delighted. He fired Bruce.

* * * * *

Bruce's recommendations, which were basically sound, were years ahead of the aspirations of a young, untried democracy. But, if accepted, they could have been the first step toward an independent, but loyal country. The Bruce Report failed because the backing by Sam Hughes was terminated. Unfortunately, Bruce was not attuned to the British

Old Boy's Club. Sloggett had replaced Babtie, when the latter was posted to India. Jones replaced Sloggett in London, when the latter was sent to France to resolve a problem. Both the Red Cross and St. John's Ambulance felt that they were capable of tending battlefield casualties and there was little need for the RAMC. Sloggett established the primacy of the RAMC, and was in no mood to accept any recommendation, from a colonial, which would reduce RAMC leadership. Bruce's gumption in challenging the establishment showed he had learned well from his old mentor, Sir Frederick Treves, who had confronted the Boer War brass.

Hughes, in spite of all the pejoratives hurled at him by party and non-party members, might well have been the right man for that time. His quarter-hour of fame was cut short by a false premise: Hughes did not bring the Ross rifle into the arsenal. It was favoured by the previous Minister of Defence, Frederick Borden. Hughes, who was under investigation regarding munition procurement by the Shell Committee, was exonerated. However the implications during the hearing and his backing of the unsuitable Ross were enough for Prime Minister Borden to open the exit door.

The same enthusiasm that roared against Catholics, raised the first contingent. The same brashness that assailed Imperial brass hats, assaulted the closed colonial mind-set of Canadians. The same rhetoric which outraged friends and foe, mobilized a people that slumbered in security. If Vimy was the birth of a nation, Hughes was one of the attendants. And the accoucheur did not leave the delivery room. When Lieut-General Arthur Currie ordered the attack on Mons, with full knowledge that there was to be an Armistice, Hughes in the House of Commons stated that this needless sacrifice of the lives of Canadians warranted trial and conviction by a court-martial.

The Bruce report resulted in many unattributed changes, which were implemented even up to WWII. His code of honour did not permit any gratuitous criticsm of Jones, but Perley was considered to be the nemesis.

Bruce was hurt by what he considered an unwarranted interference by Osler. However the Inspector General did not give way to the mighty Sir William — a pattern which was cut for future encounters with authorities.

The re-evaluation of both Hughes and Bruce awaited many years.

NOTES

1. Manion, R. J. *A Surgeon in Arms*. McClelland, Goodchild & Stewart, 1918: 116.
2. The Perley Papers, Archives of Ontario, contain the originals of the letters cited in this chapter.
3. Queen's University Archives contain the originals of Bruce's correspondence with Beaverbrook and Hughes.

CHAPTER 6

Retreat from a Battlefield

It seems to me that at present there is no further need of a Special Inspector-General of Medical Services, and I have therefore decided to relieve you of the duties of that office, to which you were appointed by the Honourable Sir Sam Hughes, K.C.B., when he was Minister of Militia and Defence. I have also decided to withdraw at the same time, the authority given to you through Major-General J. W. Carson, under which the management and control of the Medical Services were handed to you and the acting Director of M.S. was to take his instructions and orders from you. Will you kindly hand over the books and papers connected with your office to Colonel Murray MacLaren, A/D.M.S.

Thanking you for the attention which you have given to your duties.

I am, yours very truly,

George H. Perley

Bruce laid down and bled awhile, and then got up to fight again. He cleared his desk by advising Perley to authorize travel warrants and expenses involved in the inspection of the Canadian sick and wounded in Imperial Hospitals. This had been ongoing during the Inquiry and it was necessary that the amount should be passed for payment when certified. Perley approved. Bruce had a conversation, conducted in formal tones, with Perley when he suggested that Bruce accept a post as Consulting Surgeon to some hospitals in France under the British War Office. Bruce declined. He stated that he considered it was his duty to the Canadian sick and wounded to launch an appeal to the Canadian public. Following that refusal, Bruce had a conversation with Beaverbrook, who had communicated with Perley, and "...with eloquence and his well known persuasive powers, he has induced me to postpone my departure in the hope that an adjustment may be arrived at. I am now prepared to accept your offer of the position of Consulting Surgeon to some hospitals in France under the British War Office, provided that I am given the rank of Surgeon-General in the Canadian Army Medical Corps. In conclusion, I will not go into the compelling reasons which Aitken advanced, except to mention that he bases his arguments entirely on patriotic grounds."

Perley felt pressured and explained on the January 11 that he was unable to offer such a post as it rested with the British War Office. "However I felt and still feel that your skill and experience would be of great value in that work and I did say to you that I would submit your name as a Consulting Surgeon if you were prepared to accept such a position, which is certainly a very important one, filled only by men of the highest professional standing."

The two men bargained by mail over the next few days, but Perley did not reveal a letter he had received from Sir Alfred Keogh, K.C.B., Surgeon General Army Medical Services, War Office, which stated:

...there are objections to Bruce. The attitude which Colonel Bruce has assumed towards

Canadian, and indeed Imperial Medical Administration, makes it by no means certain that his employment as a consultant would be very effective, while the tendency which he has displayed to examine and criticize branches of work with which he is, from want of training, unfamiliar, might again lead to friction, which, with an army on service, might lead to serious consequences. It would be well, therefore, I think, if you would make another selection from amongst the well-known Canadian surgeons.

This letter ambushed Perley and he was forced into the situation of replying "I am sorry, but it is too late to withdraw the consent which you told me you were prepared to give to the appointment of Colonel Bruce."

Finally, Bruce withdrew his demand for a higher rank, accepting the position of Consulting Surgeon, because of patriotic feelings and because "...the question of rank means nothing to me."

While Perley may have had a secret agenda in insuring that Bruce remained in uniform, thus the offer of an appointment with the RAMC, Bruce claimed at a later date that his resignation had been refused and in addition that Perley had requested him to sign a statement that "I did not mean certain things which I had said in my report."

By this time the whole story was flooding Canadian newspapers. The original Bruce report had been "leaked," possibly by Hughes, prior to his resignation as Minister of Militia. By January 6, 1917, *The Financial Post* reported the sweeping recommendations that Bruce had made and that the Board of Inquiry had taken exception to his criticisms and exonerated the heads of services on most points and concurred with Bruce only on certain minor recommendations. *The Globe* characterized this story as being a medical controversy, which should serve as a lesson to those laymen who were apt to be "...influenced by the modern dogma of the infallibility of doctors." Bruce continued to make his case with Perley, objecting to the inclusion of Fotheringham, who had "...expressed himself openly and bitterly, and placed his attitude definitely on record, and is, therefore, already prejudiced."

In addition to Fotheringham, Bruce had stoutly maintained that to use members whose major activities had been in the treatment of the acutely wounded in France to judge on the administration of hospitals in England, was inappropriate.

In spite of the fact that Bruce had accused Perley of trying to "white-wash" his report, there was no hesitation in asking for special considerations. On January 22, prior to taking up his new position with the British forces, he requested special leave in order to return to Toronto to perform an important operation on Sir Lyman Melvin Jones, the manager of the Massey-Harris Company. He had seen Jones prior to coming to the U.K. the preceding year. Permission was given and he returned to Canada, avoiding any discussion of the events of the previous several months, as he was still in uniform. However, he did bolster his case against Perley by pointing out, by the King's Rules and Orders, that "...when an inquiry affects the character and military reputation of an officer or soldier, full opportunity must be afforded to the officer or soldier being present throughout the inquiry." This, of course, had not been done by the Babtie Inquiry which had, only after considerable pressure from Bruce, consented to hear his testimony. Bruce was not allowed to hear other evidence which was presented and kept hounding Perley for a transcript of the evidence. This did not arrive until well into 1917.

There was a rising sentiment that Bruce's rebuttal should be published. *The Canadian Practitioner and Review* on March 17 and again in September held a strong view that it should be made public. *The Halifax Observer* printed a pro-Bruce editorial under the heading, "Some Medical History." *The Globe* on several occasions talked about the pros and cons of "segregation" mainly in terms of costs versus the welfare of the soldier. *The Canadian Practitioner and Review* felt that neither Jones nor Bruce were the culprits but rather Sam Hughes himself should be held responsible.

The Medical Press and Circular followed the line taken by *Saturday Night* in attacking the chairman, Sir William Babtie. Although he had been cleared by a Parliamentary Inquiry at Westminster, there was still a strong feeling that he was responsible for the debacle at the Khut, and should never have been appointed as Head of a Board which was investigating another officer. This was in line with Bruce's objection that Babtie had been chosen, after Osler had refused, at the suggestion of the Imperial Staff. The other members of the committee were picked by Perley. None of them had practical experience of hospital administration, particularly in the U.K., and therefore were not competent to sit in judgment. The rapidity with which the Board reached a decision indicated that there was minimal on-site inspection to test the validity of Bruce's criticisms.

Of course most of these matters did not come out until the fall of 1917. In May, Bruce wrote a letter to the Honourable J. D. Reid, MP, Minister of Customs, in which he lamented the fact that his rebuttal had not been published. In addition, he wrote,

"I cannot believe that the Canadian government approves of the treatment accorded me by Sir George Perley and I do not at present feel disposed to hold it responsible. Perley is too weak and uninformed to reach a decision by himself and, as a consequence, is entirely in the hands of a clique of expatriate Canadians in London, mostly women, who tell him what to do. ...certain recommendations, for example, concentration of Canadian patients in our own hospital, were objected to by one or two women in London and in order to satisfy them and to save the reputation of the man responsible for the shortcomings in the Medical Service, a Board was carefully selected for the purpose of white-washing my report... ."

Bruce was referring to a meeting he had attended at which Lady Drummond, Lady Perley and other ladies voiced vehement opinions to Perley and Jones.

During his recent visit to Toronto and Ottawa, in order to operate on Lyman Jones, Bruce had been asked by an executive member of a Conservative organization in Toronto, if he would accept the nomination at the next election, and "I promised" to do so. "My reason for being willing to offer myself as a candidate for Parliament is that there would be many medical problems for consideration after this war, that my experience may be of some value in helping to solve. I have always been a Conservative and I cannot allow any individual like Perley, who for some accountable reason (certainly not for his ability) has been placed temporarily in a position of authority, which he has improperly used, to cause me to a break with my party." However, his political intentions were questioned by Beaverbrook as soon as he heard of them through the grapevine. He fired off a letter to Bruce strongly urging him not to accept the Tory nomination in North Toronto.

Beaverbrook was under considerable stress at that time, what with his duties in the war effort and his physical condition. Bruce, after consulting with Dr. J. F. Jennings, suggested that Beaverbrook should have a barium swallow to determine the basis of his gastro-intestinal complaints. The up-shot, as Jennings predicted, "What a difficult man he is to treat. My own feeling is that if he would submit to a course of treatment, if he would lead a rather different life, his digestion could be quite readily cured."

During his Toronto visit for the operation Bruce had an opportunity to inspect the rather woeful status of military hospitals in the Toronto area. The first had been established in 1914 at Exhibition Camp but it was moved to a tent hospital in Niagara in 1915. When the need for hospital accommodation became more acute, a Military Hospital Commission was established, and by November 1915 the old Bishop Strachan school on College Street was fitted with the necessary equipment. By the spring of 1916 more accommodation was required so the old Toronto General Hospital on Gerrard Street became a base hospital. Meanwhile, Camp Borden opened a hospital unit. In April 1916 Mrs. H. D. Warren donated the use of her house at the corner of Wellesley and Jarvis as an officer's convalescent home, and later Charles M. Beatty donated his home in York Mills for the Royal Flying Corps.

But the demand increased, particularly after Bruce's recommendations that casualties should not be treated in England for any length of time, but should be sent back to Canada. The result of this was that Givens Street school was taken over, the Burnside Pavilion at the Toronto General was set aside for infectious cases, and The Women's Pavilion for surgical cases.

Meanwhile, subsequent to Bruce's recommendations with regard to venereal disease among enlisted men, plans were made to treat all such "casualties," contracted in Canada, at Camp Borden. Bruce had already recommended that VD cases should not be treated in the front lines or in back-up hospitals but in special units which would include physical training and drill. However, long-term cases, particularly those associated with gonorrheal arthritis, were invalided back to Canada. Bruce had been shocked at the high percentage — 28.7 per cent — of troops that were infected. This was much higher than the Australians and New Zealanders and more than the British troops. Part of this disparity could be explained by the fact that the British had contacts who were non-infective. However the frustrating statistic for Bruce was the number of men who arrived in England with the disease, although the standard lectures for soldiers' "wholesome activities" organized by the YMCA and other preventative tactics had been used in Canada.[1] This statistic must have caused consternation to Robert Borden, who in 1917 stated, "I say un-hestitantly that if I should be Prime Minister of Canada on the outbreak of another war, I would not send one man overseas if the condition were such that prevailed during the progress of this war... I am absolutely astonished that no steps of any reasonable adequate character have been taken here to prevent these women swarming around our camps all over this kingdom."

The devastating toll of VD among fighting men continued even with the best efforts of prevention. The Imperial Army was of the opinion that issuing condoms led to promiscuity. The Americans and other colonies issued prevention packets consisting of potassium permanganate and calomile, but many soldiers refused to use them. The Canadians set up early-treatment centres in cities throughout Britain and penalized infected soldiers. Part of the difficulty in solving the problem was a disagreement among the higher-ups. Some felt that promiscuity was encouraged by providing methods of combating infections. Others opined that the punishment for contracting VD was so severe that it would discourage soldiers from reporting. The British even went so far as to state that under extreme mental tension, it was permissible to masturbate; however, this was not to be done for enjoyment.[2]

To Jack Canuck in the trenches, there was constant dilemma. On the one hand was the purposeful blind ignorance to the problem as expressed by Dr. Andrew Macphail of McGill: "Their chastity was absolute, for the battalion remained for a whole year in a place from which the civilian population had been completely evacuated."[3] On the other hand, Osler's article in the *BMJ* pointed out that there was no clear record of venereal statistics and that "...war meant an enormous increase in a number of infections. In the Canadian Army there had been enough cases of venereal disease to stir public opinion in the Dominion to the boiling point."[4]

One of the confounding factors in the problems associated with sexuality was a communication taken from a German prisoner, captured near Ypres-Comines Canal on March 2, 1916.

Translation of a German document dated 20/2/16.

(Taken from a German Prisoner captured near the Ypres-Comines Canal, March 2nd, 1916.)

"Committee for the increase of the Population".
                                    Notice No. 138756.

Sir,————————

On account of all the able-bodied men having been called to the Colours, it remains the duty of all those left behind, for the sake of the Fatherland, to interest themselves in the happiness of the married women and maidens by doubling or even trebling the number of births.

Your name has been given to us as a capable man, and you are herewith requested to take on this office of honour and to do your duty in a proper German way. It must here be pointed out that your wife or fiancee will not be able to claim a divorce; it is in fact to be hoped that the women will bear this discomfort heroically for the sake of the war.

You will be given the district of .... Should you not feel capable of carrying on the task allotted to you, you will be given three days in which to name someone in your place. On the other hand, if you are prepared to take on a second district as well, you will become a "Deckoffizier" and receive a pension.

An exhibition of photographs of women and maidens in the district allotted to you is to be found at the office of .... You are requested to bring this letter with you.

Your good work should commence immediately on this notification. A full report of results is to be submitted by you after 9 months.[5]

Macphail had an alternative idea of prevalence and

suggested the possibility that there was a lower incidence of venereal disease in certain troops "...may be
that many of the men contracted in civil life that form
of venereal disease which afterwards confers immu-
nity, and also that other form which when it recurs
may be almost negligible."[6]

With termination of his position as IG, Bruce began
to close down his office. MacLaren remained as
Acting Director and lost no time in requesting Bruce
to turn over "...all files and documents and reports of
inspections of Canadian patients in British hospitals." These were not in the office. By the next day
MacLaren notified the Adjutant-General that the matter of handling over the files and other documents
had not been completed and he was awaiting a
signed document from Bruce that all documents had
been transferred.

Bruce now demonstrated that he had indeed
learned the "army way." He began a series of nitpick-
ing memos and languorous letters. MacLaren
demanded why 55 travel warrants had been unaccounted for and requested that all unused warrants
be returned as well as particulars of those that had
been used. Bruce responded that the warrants were
handled by an officer and subsequently an NCO and
he had no particular knowledge of the warrants. He
added that he had handed over certain files and documents to MacLaren but other documents and
papers had been given to the secretary of the Board
of Inquiry. He had retained papers of a personal
nature and also copies of documents which he proposed to keep relating to his appointment, etc.
MacLaren was then in touch with Headquarters,
pointing out that papers were being retained and
warrants that were unaccounted. The Adjutant-
General sent a gentle note to Bruce requesting com-

pliance. Bruce answered by sending certain records and files etc. and giving further explanations regarding the warrants. This led to a letter from the Adjutant-General to Bruce on the 10th of December requesting (!) that he report to Headquarters in order that the GOC might see him. At the same time MacLaren sent a letter to the Director of Medical Services, complaining that 17 files had not been returned and it was not understood why all copies of correspondence and documents had been withheld. This caused a prompt letter from the Adjutant-General to Bruce requesting him to communicate with the Director of Medical Services with regard to the missing 17 files. This number dropped to thirteen over the next few days. In addition the Director of Medical Services requested all copies of correspondence. Bruce replied that the thirteen files were single letters of no materiality, and one file that had been requested had been returned to Perley. The problem was resolved when the Adjutant-General suggested to Perley that they accept Bruce's statements and not pursue the matter any further. It was a clear wear-down win for Bruce. Then in this classic example of one grasshopper jumping upon another grasshopper's back, Bruce requested the return of certain files. The Attorney General ruled this out as they were the property of the Medical Department. Bruce explained in a letter to Beaverbrook that he was anxious to retain certain documents in case he decided to mount a legal action in the future.

On Bruce's return to France, he was seconded to the Royal Army Medical Corps and began his surgical duties. He left Toronto before the March 10, 1917, issue of *The Financial Post* which contained the rebuttal report which Bruce had made to the Babtie Board, which had been accepted by Perley but had not been circulated. Somehow *The Financial Post* received a copy, possibly from the same source that had leaked the original Bruce Report to Hughes.

The Post stated that the rebuttal re-opened the whole question of administration of the Canadian Medical Services in Great Britain. It took credit for publishing the first report which had been in response to a conviction by the paper that "the weakness of administration brought out by Colonel Bruce meant the squandering of public funds and the piling up of heavy debts to be liquidated by the taxpayers after the war."

The newspaper charged that the Babtie Board dismissed many of Bruce's findings as "minor" matters but *The Post* disagreed and felt that they were ".... paramount rather than minor importance inasmuch as they dealt with the wholesale acceptance of unfit recruits and the lack of adequate inspection."

The reporter acutely observed that the conflict between Bruce and Perley developed from the fact that Sam Hughes had stood behind Bruce, and Perley had contested Hughes on the matter of caring for the Canadian wounded. "So great was the desire of Sir George Perley to prevent a full and frank statement of the situation from being made public in Canada, that steps were actually taken with a view to preventing Colonel Bruce from returning to Canada at all," stated *The Post.*

Bruce did not receive copies of this until August, and then forwarded it to Beaverbrook. He also gave an account of his activities over the previous few weeks. He had visited General Currie at Canadian Headquarters and suggested that he might be of help in a Casualty Clearing Station (CCS). The response was enthusiastic and he arrived on the 29th of July and during the following two days operated continuously for 16 hours a day and on the third day 12 hours. Following that he visited No. 13 CCS in the neighbourhood and performed many operations. He was filled with pride at the work of the stretcher bearers in collecting the wounded, at great personal risk. He ended the letter by pointing out he was disappointed that the government had not laid his reply on the table but felt that his friends, including Victor Ross, of Imperial Oil and a long-time conservative, would take care of the omission.

He also discussed the question whether he would return to Canada and participate in the election but left the decision on that to Victor Ross and Dalton McCarthy. He had received a letter from Dr. Allan of the Executive Committee of the Conservative Association of North Toronto stating that he would have no difficulty in defeating the Liberal candidate. Bruce replied that if he accepted the nomination it would be with the understanding that he was free to criticize the action of Perley over the past several months. If the convention objected to his attitude then he would run as an independent conservative.

On October 21 in another letter to Beaverbrook he recounted that he had continued with many operations including on Canadians and had been "very busy." In addition to inquiring as to Beaverbrook's health and whether the X-ray examination had been performed, he went on to discuss the election. He had declined the Allan invitation to accept the nomination on the strong advice of Sir William Mulock, McCarthy, and Ross. He did this largely because the question of conscription overshadowed every other issue at the present moment and he felt it would be an unfavourable time to ventilate the abuses in the medical situation. Beaverbrook was barely mollified that Bruce had taken a Liberal's advice, when it was explained it was on the basis of a long friendship.

Bruce also added his delight that Perley had been moved from his position.

Beaverbrook was adamant that Bruce should not push for an invitation to a meeting of consulting surgeons in France, which had been called, and to which he had not been invited. Although Bruce had suggested to Sloggett that it would be appropriate for him to go, as he was the only Canadian in the area, Beaverbrook did not feel that he should ask for even small favours until his whole situation with the Canadian Medical Services was clarified. There was no doubt that Bruce was being accepted with open arms by the RAMC and was active as one of the 12 surgical consultants in the Le Havre and Deauville hospital area. This entailed not only operating and giving advice but regular meetings with the other eleven surgical consultants and the Director of Medical Services to discuss various problems. During August and September of 1917 Bruce was put in charge of a CCS set aside for the treatment of head injuries. He consulted with Dr. Harvey Cushing, another trainee of Horsley, who was in an adjoining CCS station. It was there that Revere Osler, Sir William's son, died on August 31, 1917. He was buried the next day.

> A soggy Flanders field beside a little oak grove to the rear of the Dosingham Group — an overcast, windy, calm, autumnal day — the long rows of simple wooden crosses — the new ditches half-full of water being dug by Chinese Coolies wearing tin helmets — the boy wrapped in an army blanket and covered by a weather-worn Union Jack, carried on their shoulders by four slipping stretcher bearers. A strange scene — the great-great-grandson of Paul Revere under the British

flag, and awaiting him a group of some 6 or 8 American Army medical officers saddened with the thoughts of his father.[7]

In March of 1918 the French Army Medical Organization asked Bruce to make a tour and make suggestions for improvements. He travelled with Dr. George Crile of Cleveland and visited many hospital centres.

This was followed by a mission for the British Government to the USA to address the American Medical Association meeting in Chicago and the Medical Surgical Association in Cincinnati. His travelling companions were two eminent Englishmen, Sir William Arbuthnot Lane and Sir James MacKenzie. Lane was Surgeon to the Queen and had many credits to his name including internal fixation of fractures. He was also famous for his hemi-colectemy operations which were performed on the basis of preventing the pooling of toxic materials in the large intestine. He had visited The Wellesley Hospital prior to the war, when he demonstrated his "no touch" technique of aseptic operations to Bruce. Sir James MacKenzie, a world eminent physician had described the condition known as "soldier's heart," which was the basis for many discharges from the service. This was not the first time that Bruce had made a military visit to the U.S. In 1916 had been invited by Newton Baker, Secretary of War, to visit Washington, D.C., and address the Council of National Defence on the subject of Medical Organization in the armed forces.

On return to duty at Le Havre, by a strange series of coincidences, he met a young VAD, Amy Augusta Hall, who was in charge of the VAD residence for the Number 2 General Hospital. "After many years of bachelorhood, instinct told me that at last I'd seen the girl that I wished to marry. It was a clear case of love at first sight!"[8] A further meeting was enhanced by the presence of Canon J. Cody of St. Paul's Church, Toronto, who was also Minister of Education for Ontario. Bruce arranged a tour of the area for Cody and ended up at Number 2 General Hospital; he insured that his minister could meet Amy and bear witness to his character. Bruce became a frequent visitor to the hospital, on official business of course, over the next several months.

The war ended in November and Bruce was in a stew to propose and marry Amy. But she was on the French side of the channel and it was difficult to get transportation, unless there was top priority. Fortunately Bruce was able to generate a telegram informing that Amy Augusta Hall's mother was seriously ill and the VAD required special transport papers. The information was accepted as factual and she arrived in London.

The only disappointment was that the recommendation that Bruce be knighted for his services — as were all other colonels in the RAMC — was vetoed by General Foster as "not approved."

The escape from France was rapid, and it was followed by a whirlwind marriage at St. Margaret's Church, the chapel to the House of Commons in Westminster. Amy gazed at her 49-year-old groom — at his patrician features, his keen blue eyes, and his prematurely white hair. He was an outstandingly handsome man who wore his civilian clothes in the same elegant way as his uniform. Neat, crisp, and well turned out. Her dark-haired beauty was set-off by the white wedding gown. There were only a few guests. The bride's family came down from Upminster. Amy's father, a mining engineer, frequently worked in Chile, where Amy Augusta was born. (She changed her name to Angela for the wedding ceremony, and also upgraded her birthplace from Chile to England.)

The best man was an old friend of Herbert's, Sir George Badgerow, and the other witness was Dr. R. J. Macmillan. Amy had known Macmillan since he had arrived in France after a smooth sailing, but stormy passage. This paradox was due to the Army flak he received on disembarking. He had volunteered to join Bruce in the RAMC, but the Canadian authorities pointed out that since he was in the Reserve of the Canadian Militia, he could not be transferred without permission. In addition he had travelled to England without authorization. His association with Bruce did not make the paper flow more efficiently, but eventually he did join the RAMC. His allegiance to Bruce was clear, since he had been on the staff of the pre-war Wellesley Hospital.

The honeymoon was at Cherkely, where Beaverbrook had entertained them before the wedding. On one occasion he had pulled the bride-to-be aside, saying, "I suppose you know you are marrying a very rich man?" Angela replied that she had no particular interest in money. Beaverbrook, who handled Bruce's finances, knew of his fortune, which had started with his surgical fees, and quickly mounted with shrewd investments.

Actually, Beaverbrook should have been at the wedding, but a few months previously he had noticed a swelling around his neck and had entreated Bruce to come. The diagnosis was actinomycosis and he was started on a course of iodine to reduce the swelling. The day before the wedding Beaverbrook begged Bruce to take a train to Eastbourne for a repeat examination. The urgent invitation was accompanied by a train schedule which showed that it could be done, all in time for the nuptials.

Fortunately, the trains were true to schedule and Bruce reached the church on time.

Beaverbrook had an operation for the fungus in February with Bruce assisting Mr. Wilfrid Trotter, who had been in the same post-graduate course at the Royal College. While visiting the recuperating patient, Herbert and Angela were asked to remain to meet the Prime Minister, David Lloyd George, who, after some government business was completed, turned to Mrs. Bruce and asked about her war service. Lloyd George always had an eye for young women, and Angela knew the music hall tune, "Lloyd George knew my mother." She was proud to report that she earned a second proficiency stripe after two years overseas service in the VAD and had been mentioned in dispatches by Sir Douglas Haig. She confided that she had wanted to be a VAD early in the war, but had been too young. So she had taken a poultry course but gave that up and eventually did enter the VAD, and went to France as the youngest to go to the continent. However, she overestimated her strength and had to leave the bedside activity, and was relegated to House Mother to other VADs, which consisted of cooking and housekeeping activities. Meanwhile, she had been introduced to Bruce, who was stationed nearby. His visits became more frequent and were sometimes garnished with small Fortnum and Mason's basket suppers. Later, he invited her to dine in nearby restaurants. He proposed to her just before the Armistice and possibly sensing her hesitation at the age difference, appeared with a friend, Canon Cody, who was touring the front. The cleric was able to assure the young VAD, by look and touch, that Herbert was a good match.

* * * * *

Bruce vindicated himself by his work with the RAMC. His surgical skills were clearly apparent and his administrative abilities were recognized by his posting to the U.S.A. and secondment to the French Army. During this time he avoided any public discussion of his problems with the Canadian authorities.

He handled himself well on the battlefields of France and was also adept in the London bureaucracy. The dodging game he played with Perley's staff in hiding documents, which might be needed in the future, was supplemented by persuading office staff to copy, illicitly, all pertinent communications and pass them on to a friend, who carried the documents to Toronto. Captain Charles "Chubby" Power proved to be a reliable courier, and went on to become a Liberal cabinet minister.

The whirlwind romance with Amy Augusta was not in character for the surgeon, who carefully planned his activities, and could be explained only, in his own words, as "love at first sight".

NOTES

1. Bates, G. "Venereal Diseases from the Preventative Aspects." *CMAJ* 1919: 9: 310-18.

2. Cassel, J. *The Secret Plague: Venereal Disease in Canada 1838-1939*. University of Toronto Press, 1987: 122-44.

3. Macphail, A. *Official History of the Canadian Forces in the Great War 1914-919*. Ottawa, 1925: 292.

4. *BMJ*, May 26, 1917: 695.

5. Robertson, A. Irvine. Official Papers WW1. 1915-16: Archives of Ontario. MU4113.

6. Macphail, op.cit., 293.

7. Cushing, H. *From a Surgeon's Journal 1915-18*, Constable, 1936: 98.

8. Bruce, H. A. *Varied Operations*: Longmans, Green, 1958: 101.

   All quotes from letters and reports are from the Perley Papers, Archives of Ontario, or the Bruce Papers, Queen's University Archives.

CHAPTER 7

One More Inquiry

It was a regal reception. Nurses lined the burnished corridors and bobbed when presented by Elsie Flaws to Mrs. Bruce. The second day in Toronto was a mounting series of pleasures as Angela met Herbert's many friends, professional and social, culminating with Sir William Mulock.

This was a most agreeable change to the cramped passage across the Atlantic on the troopship *S.S. Malita* with hundreds of returning soldiers, and a few war brides. But at least Herbert had been able to get two berths, because of the urgency to return to his practice. The first view of the country at St. John, New Brunswick, in March was devastating — so cold, so much snow — but warmth awaited the following morning when they were met at Union Station in Toronto by the Mayor, Tommy Church.

There were few royals in Toronto, but the local Debrett's, The Toronto Society Blue Book and Club List, lost little time in turning out to see the bride of the famous surgeon, who had been a very eligible bachelor. Ever since he had managed to avoid entanglement with any of the three daughters in the home where he had usually taken Sunday dinner, while a student, there had been occasional whiffs of liaisons, but no smoke ever emerged to suggest there had been any fire. He was as determined in his work, as he was to avoid marriage. Still, there were rumours!

Angela soon realized that she had married well. The

Bruce home purchased in 1908, at the northwest corner of Bloor and Church streets, was extensive. Besides commodious day rooms, there was a wing for his office, which included a nurse and two secretaries, one of whom was multi-lingual and translated articles for the library. In addition there were tennis courts, garages, and stables.

The house staff, which had been kept on while Bruce was away, were delighted that the residence was alive again and readily turned to preparing dinner parties, frequently for up to twenty guests. Two of the staff, the Hard sisters, had been part of a family in Port Perry and had worked in Stewart Bruce's house. When Bruce's mother, Isabel, became ill, he rushed up from Toronto and met the sisters before she died. He gave his mother a promise that he would look after them and brought both back to the Bloor street house, where one worked as a cook and the other laid out his clothes. In addition to receptions, which introduced Angela to The Blue Book, there were return invitations to Sir John Eaton's, where she first heard a radio, and to the Riddells and Cawthras. Some of these happenings were recorded by Miss Beatrice Sullivan, who wrote a social column for the *Mail and Empire*, arbitrarily separating those who wanted their presence mentioned, from those who preferred to merge with the drapes.

Meanwhile Bruce returned to his busy work schedule. However, one task took priority. He had held any further counter-attacks against Perley and the High Command until he was out of uniform. On Civvy street he had no difficulty in recruiting Hector Charlesworth of *Saturday Night* to write a foreword for a polemic which, after citing numerous supporting documents, claimed vindication of the Bruce Report. The fact that Bruce had lied to the staff, who had accepted his word that all the papers had been returned, was infuriating to the War Office.

The publication, *Politics and the C.A.M.C.*, 1919, revived suspicions that there had been a concerted attempt to paper-over gaping cracks in the administration of the Medical Services, with terrible consequences for Canadian casualties. There was little new in the book. The main outcome was that it strung together all the letters and telegrams that had kept many people at the War Office busy during the disagreement.

An anonymous critic at Headquarters stated there was much in Bruce's book, "...to which no exceptions can be taken, such as record of letters and exchanges with various persons, the record of reports... But even a great surgeon is not always free from the mental obliquity which warps judgment... which interprets any interference with his plans, every dissent from his views as the offspring of jealousy and a product of personal prejudices." There followed a line-by-line dissection of the book, pointing out where there was not agreement.

The newspapers quickly pumped up the charges made in Bruce's book, concluding that it was essentially a defence of his recommendations, an indictment of the Babtie Report, and a condemnation of Perley. "A strange tale of sensational allegations on which Sir George Perley is under attack," said one paper. The author stated that "a hand-picked commission had been secured to pass on the report." However, the reaction was not one-sided. "Without military experience, other than obtained in a few weeks spent in 1915, it seemed scarcely credible that any man would have the effrontery to undertake such a task," said another.

This flurry of interest was given added fillip by

Brigadier-General C. A. Smart, CMG, a Conservative member in the Quebec legislature who delivered a blistering criticism of Perley and the administration of the Medical Service on March 15, 1919. He was "...as good an Imperialist as anybody else, but he did not maintain it at the cost of wounded men," and he accused the administration of favouritism, with concrete examples of mal-administration. He moved a motion expressing the opinion of the Provincial Legislature that the Federal Government should release full information to the public. "I say without fear of contradiction from any impartial source, that the medical administration has been bad."

Smart's credentials were sound — he had been CO at Shorncliffe and had also administered seven other hospitals. He continued: "Practically every recommendation made by Colonel Bruce that was turned down by the Committee had since been adopted and put into effect."

The pot was beginning to simmer. Smart's charges were answered in the Federal House by Sir Thomas White, who took the approach that the Brigadier-General's pique was caused by the lack of pips. He wanted a promotion. It all made for interesting journalism. Lieutenant-Colonel Arthur Clarence Pratt in the Ontario Legislature brought the pot to a boil with more comments on the inadequacy of the administration "...bungling, uncommon, discourteous men."

The government was anxious to contain the uproar and felt that, "The newspapers are greatly to blame for listening to the tittle-tattle of every returned man who fancies he has a grievance," at the time of the arrival of Major F. J. Ewing at Halifax. He gave an interview, "I could tell you stories about that place (Canadian Headquarters) that would make your hair stand, but I won't on account of my present position."

The criticism was becoming more alarming to the senior government members, and Osler suggested that three eminent surgeons who had just returned to Canada should make countering statements. However, Perley shushed him with an "I don't take seriously articles in the papers."

The *Toronto Globe* may have been privy to Osler's letter because it presented an interview with

a prominent citizen who, although un-named, undoubtedly expresses the view among officers returning from the Front and civilians who had the opportunity of personal observation... There has been developing among many of our soldiers waiting to be conveyed home, a most regrettable feeling of bitterness. ...I found the most unfortunate feeling existing among the private soldiers towards the overseas Canadian administration. They feel that Sir Edward Kemp and Sir George Perley are so engrossed in their social duties and aspirations that they have little time for the consideration of the Canadian soldier. This is all part of the campaign against Perley, undoubtedly launched by Bruce, through Charlesworth.

However the heat beneath some collars was blistering the chairs of some of the bureaucrats. General Foster was satisfied that there would be a complete repudiation of many of the charges, however "I carefully considered the matter and took it up with Fotheringham and Sir Andrew Macphail... Sir Andrew expressed himself as willing to do anything in this matter, to write a book that you might desire, but he expressed that he could not see flogging a dead horse, but if there be further developments, it may become necessary to come up with a book, such

as we discussed, for the public." Although the whole
story had been well chewed over at many dinner
tables and in the officers' mess, there was still sufficient meat left, that a decision was made to proceed
with a publication by MacPhail.

Bruce had now returned to increased activities in
the operating room and was doing a tremendous
amount of work. Angela reported that it was not
unusual for the telephone to ring for the doctor while
they were at dinner; however, she put her foot down
and dinner-time ringing was banned. He did however,
upon occasion, leave the table, "just for a short
spell," and returning in half an hour having performed an appendectomy.

He continued to make many speeches including a
description of the new artificial legs and arms which
had been developed by Putti of Bologna. These
devices for amputees used a type of tendon contrac-
tion to open and close prosthetic hands. Bruce was
enthusiastic about their possibilities, particularly for
amputee veterans in Canada. During the question
period after a lecture he was asked whether Canada
was a fertile field for soldiers returning from England
who might bring some Bolshevik ideas with them.
Bruce denied there was and asserted that he was
quite confident that Bolshevism would be expelled
from England, as Lloyd George would be taking
strong measures to put it down.

In addition to speaking on medical matters, Bruce
gave several political addresses supporting the
Honourable Mr. Arthur Meighen who had been
accused of offering bribes to the electorate. In one
speech the doctor spoke of the tremendous development of industry in the United States saying that
there was no middle ground for Canada. "She must
take such steps that will guarantee her self-preserva-

tion and concern herself in what is after all her best product — her boys and girls — or she must acknowledge herself content to play the position of handmaiden and bond servant to American interest, supplying brain power and raw materials."

Another of his addresses described the advances that had been made in blood transfusion. Dr. Lawrence Bruce Robertson graduated from the U of T in 1910 and went overseas in 1915. Working in No. 2 CCS, he invented a machine that would draw blood from a donor and keep it cool so that it was available to transfuse into a casualty. This type of exsanguination transfusion was the beginning of a series of advances of transfusing blood, using citrates and eventually storing the donor blood. Bruce pointed out that on many occasions he had seen Robertson taking blood from "strapping young soldiers" who were near a casualty centre and passing it directly into a wounded soldier. It saved many lives.

The procedures were demonstrated to the Imperial Forces which adopted them enthusiastically. Following the war, Robertson returned to Toronto and pioneered a procedure for children whereby he drew off "toxic" blood and replaced it with the pure blood of healthy people.

The war of words continued. It was an excellent lesson from which opponents of the government, past and present, could score points, but no clear victory was declared for either side. Bruce let his friends do the campaigning as he was absorbed more and more in his practice, and then too, he had a son. Herbert Maxwell Bruce was born at home on February 24th, 1920. It was an easy birth, but was complicated by post-delivery infection; the boy remained the only child. Meanwhile Bruce and Angela had discovered an ideal building site on the east side of Bayview

Avenue, fallen in love with it, and hired an English
architect and a Scottish landscaper to build
"Annandale," taking the name from the estate in
Scotland which had been given by King David I to
Robert de Brus. There was a good barn in the
meadow beside the Don River, and Bruce began an
Ayrshire herd, whose milk was most digestible for
infants.

Like the Bloor Street residence it soon became the
centre for entertaining a list of distinguished visitors.
One occasion included Sir Ernest Shackelton, who
was touring the country searching for funds for his
Antarctica explorations. They spent a merry evening
recalling Perkins Bull and his shenanigans in
Shackelton's old home in Putney. The polar explorer
received a frigid welcome from John Eaton to a suggestion that funds from that dinner guest would
result in any new discovery being named after the
department-store mogul.

Most of the dinner guests were made up of judges
and lawyers, plus overseas visitors. Viscount
Birkenhead, one-time Lord Chancellor of England,
was able to quote so impressively from his library,
that later Bruce purchased a good deal of it from the
estate.

Sam Hughes, who was still active in the House,
dined frequently. He had lost none of the frankness
of irresponsibility and frequently outraged the more
socially squeamish, who winced during his tirades.
There were a few, not including Angela, who were
sensitive to terms such as "Jew" and "nigger"; and
various religious sects were frequent targets of scorn.
It was almost enough to break up an evening when
Sam was at full gallop, but there was always the
excuse that, of course, any person who led the
Orange Parade on a white horse on the glorious 12th

could be tolerated, if not forgiven. He was rapidly becoming a caricature of the over-zealous and under-endowed.

Crossing the Atlantic was almost a routine activity for Bruce; in 1923 the family was welcomed in London by W. P. Larkin, now Canadian High Commissioner. En route Bruce had further conversations with Dr. Frederick Banting, who was going to Sweden to receive the Nobel Prize. Bruce wrote that Banting had cleared the air over a wide-spread controversy about the contribution of J. J. McLeod, Professor of Physiology, to the discovery of insulin. Banting stated that McLeod had shown little interest and provided only minimal facilities until the research began to be promising. From then on the communications about the earth-shaking find were referred to as "we". When McLeod gave a lecture on the subject, Charles Best was not mentioned. Banting gave half of his prize money to Best.

Arriving in England Bruce arranged, through Larkin, for Banting to be presented to the King and even helped the "...shy, young, man," to hire the necessary morning suit and silk hat from Moss Bros. Bennett, who was the next High Commissioner, was a little concerned that Banting was going through a divorce and possibly should not be presented; however, Bruce responded, "Is that anything to do with the discovery of insulin?"

Another court presentation — Angela's — was arranged by Leo Amery and Bruce's old acquaintance from Port Perry days, Florence Greenwood, who had married the famous journalist. Amery, after reporting the Boer War, where he listened to Hughes and others not in the High Command, wrote a masterly six-volume history of the struggle, which led in rapid succession to appointment as Chief Correspondent of

The Times, and then to a career in politics. He was elected to Parliament, where he alternately supported or disagreed with Winston Churchill, through Churchill's roller-coaster career. Angela received advice from Florence on how to curtsy and the two wrote to each other for many years with accounts of Leo and Florence's two sons, John and Julian.

On returning to Canada, Bruce resumed a full schedule. Many of his patients arrived from outlying towns such as Belleville, Barrie, Lindsay and Guelph, usually appearing at The Wellesley with a note saying to be admitted to a $2.50 a day bed and to call Dr. Bruce. Sometimes the surgeon and a nurse went to the patient, with Angela calling the station in the middle of the night to arrange for a special train. On other occasions the chauffeur, Kernin, whom Bruce had brought back from Europe and who doubled as a groom, cranked up the car and drove. Kernin also doubled as an operating attendant, holding one of the acetylene headlights over the patient on the kitchen table. Bruce excelled in aseptic surgery and could usually do an appendectomy in six minutes. Other procedures, such as an alcohol injection into a cranial nerve for the treatment of tic douloureux, which he learned from Harvey Cushing, required an operating room.

Although he had been head of a surgical service since 1908 at the General, he still did most his procedures at The Wellesley.

It was well that Bruce had prepared a bomb shelter in view of the Starr-shell which ignited in the spring of 1919. Sir John Eaton had gifted the Toronto General Hospital $500,000 in installments of $25,000 annually for twenty-five years. This donation was entailed in that a "full-time" professor of medicine was to be appointed, with a complete re-organization of the department. This professor was given charge of the selection of staff, the policy of teaching, and the care of the sick. It was an opportune donation as there had been talk for some time, postponed partially because of the war, that changes were required from those arrangements that had been made in the first decade of the century. The newly appointed professor got off to a running start; he abolished three co-ordinate services in medicine, forcing the retirement of well-known medical men, some of whom were still on active service overseas. These included Fotheringham, Colonel Chambers, and Major Thistle. There was some expostulation at this change with murmuring in the faculty, particularly about the appointment of a full-time professor. Osler had already turned down a similar suggestion when at Johns Hopkins. However the re-organization proceeded.

The second event was the announcement of a grant to the U of T from the Rockefeller Foundation of $1 million upon conditions which included re-organization of the Department of Surgery, similar to that which had been adopted by the Department of Medicine, and the appointment of a full-time professor. C. L. Starr, who had returned from overseas in 1918, was appointed. Since his student days when he had roomed with Bruce, he had practised outstanding surgery, and beginning in 1912 devoted himself to the Hospital for Sick Children. During the War he had been in charge of surgery at Ramsgate, England. On his appointment as surgeon-in-chief of the General he pressed on with the re-organization plans and in September of 1921 summarily dismissed from the staff Doctors Roberts, McCollum, Moorehead, and Bruce. At the same time he kept on staff two surgeons who were over the statutory age limit, Primrose and Bingham. While the changes in the Department of Medicine had caused some outcry, the entire Faculty of Medicine now hummed "...like a hive of angry bees," according to the local newspapers.

Vigorous protests were made to Starr, the Board of Trustees of the General, and the President of the University, Sir Robert Falconer. The medical and lay press entered the controversy freely, criticizing the President, the Board of Governors, and the Board of Trustees of the hospital, and the fray was joined by Colonel Thomas Gibson CMG, DSO, a U of T alumnus and Assistant Deputy Minister of Militia Overseas. He published several letters in which he claimed that men of academic distinction, who had commendable service overseas, had been promised that "...appointments equally as good and remunerative would await them on their return." So forceful was the flood of protests that the Premier E. C. Drury appointed a select committee of the Provincial Legislature to inquire into University affairs. Bruce was delighted to see that the terms of reference were enlarged considerably so that not only was the affair of the Toronto General investigated but practically all matters concerned with the University, including administration and finance, were to be examined. The small beginning had led to a comprehensive investigation. The committee was convened on October 25, 1922, and Bruce made several presentations. In his opening statement he said "I am not here in the capacity of complainant or petitioner. I have neither motives of personal ambition or personal gains to serve, nor do I feel the slightest rancour or regret of any action which has been taken affecting myself. I have come because of a sincere desire to promote the welfare of the medical faculty and of the University." He proceeded systematically to mount a case which condemned the University's actions.

He criticized Falconer for having been "...frequently unfortunate in his choice of advisors." One of these advisors, however, was beyond this criticism — it had been Bruce himself, who had stated to the President that he did not feel Starr was suitable to be appointed professor, as the major part of his work had been in the children's surgery.

One of Bruce's major targets was the manner in which the University and the General functioned with the medical staff. The arrangement had been established in 1908 and Bruce felt it to be faulty. He strongly advised that there should be an advisory committee elected from the Faculty to advise the President of the University and the Board of Trustees of the Hospital in matters of appointments and working policies. His anti-establishment bias showed clearly here, as it did with the Medical Services in WW1. He was deeply concerned that autocratic decisions were being made without adequate consultations with those who were affected. He argued strongly against the full-time professorships, and quoted the opinion of Professor John M. T. Finney, the President of the American Surgical Association, who had as recently as May 31, 1922, argued strongly against the principle. It had not been proven effective and according to Bruce, "I submit, gentlemen, that a state institution such as the University of Toronto has no place in which to spend public funds on such an experiment." He then quoted the experience from Britain where the teachers of surgery at Leeds had refused full-time professorship, when it had been proposed. His old friend Moynihan had been instrumental in this refusal. While Bruce agreed that there should be a surgeon-in-chief, he strongly advocated that the appointee should have an executive assistant who would take care of the technical matters, freeing the surgeon from the burdensome administrative tasks of running a department. The original proposition by the Rockefeller group would have limited the surgeon to a token time for private practice. Bruce urged that the appointee should be permitted to spend a maximum of three hours in any day for private work.

He disagreed and challenged a statement in favour of the Rockefeller plan by Thomas White, who was still a major figure in the operation of the General, and pointed out that White had no particular expertise in appraising a purely professional question. Similarly, he disagreed with Sir Joseph Flavelle. When the latter was testifying to the fitness of the program that had been decided by the University, Bruce challenged him with a question "...do you consider yourself competent to express a professional opinion upon how well a patient is treated for a disease from which he is suffering?" Flavelle agreed that he did not profess that at all. Bruce then built on that answer to attempt to reverse the decisions that affected patient care, and that had been made without proper representation from a Faculty Committee, which he had proposed.

There were others with whom Bruce disagreed. Nasmith testified before the committee that the major advances in medicine had been the development of laboratory medicine. Bruce quickly championed the place of the general practitioner, who frequently did not have access to, or time for, laboratory examination. He cited, with his usual sweeping statements, that he preferred to have an experienced general practitioner put his hand on a painful abdomen to

make a diagnosis of appendicitis, rather than awaiting, possibly for three days, the result of a laboratory
investigation. He urged that the art of medicine
should not surrender to the science. Of course,
Nasmith responded that the two went together.
However, Bruce was able to sway his audience, who
agreed that if one used a watch constantly, one
would lose the ability to tell the time by looking at the
sun.

After fourteen sittings the committee reported. It
believed it to be in the interests of all to have eight
elected Alumni members on the Board of Governors.
It also recommended that before any proposed gifts of
money, or plans of new buildings, the University
Senate should give approval. Currently these matters
went directly to the Board of Governors. In addressing the problem of gifts and endowments, it was felt
that "...in a publicly owned university, private
endowments should not be accepted if, attached to
them, are conditions, which would bind the university governors..." It was moved that the President
should seek the advice of a Faculty Committee before
appointing, promoting, or dismissing. It recorded its
disapproval of the re-organizations in medicine and
surgery, which "...we find to be illegal and unautho-
rized. ...that The Board of Governors and the
Trustees of the hospital respectively showed a lack of
consideration for and appreciation of the valuable
and efficient services rendered, and have abruptly
and irregularly terminated."

The committee regretted that "...the hospital staff
is controlled absolutely by the University. ...such a
condition is undesirable."

These recommendations and others bearing on the
Faculty and the University were detailed in a Draft
Bill, but the government was defeated before pas-

sage, although some of the reforms were implemented. Bruce was gratified that most of his proposals were accepted.

The fuse that had been lit previously and continued to smoulder over the years, finally ignited the powder keg and Macphail published *History of Canadian Forces, 1914–19*. Ordered in 1924, by the Privy Council, it carried the full majesty of the Department of National Defence. Macphail, K.T., O.B.E., B.A., etc., was Professor of the history of medicine, McGill University, and had been given access to the entire corpus of information of the Medical Services. The book looked in great detail at all medical activities and related them to the progress of the fighting. The Bruce affair was handled very gently, almost with forbearance in that any and all of the Special Inspector General's gross errors, misjudgements, and inaccurate assessments were blamed on his lack of military experience. In short, the interpretation of the entire affair was considered more of a tempest in a teapot, which exonerated the administration, the Babtie Committee, and Perley.

The reaction was predictable. Fotheringham proclaimed it to be a great piece of writing: "...this is not a matter of controversy, but of history. A fine dispassionate history." Nasmith, in a press interview said that it was full of errors of fact and omitted a great deal. Actually Nasmith had published *Canada's Sons and Great Britain in the World War* in 1919, a 608-page detailed history, which never once mentioned Hughes or Bruce. The latter, although he claimed that he disliked being dragged into the controversy in such detail after the war had ended, felt a response was demanded. He said, "A more unsuitable selection than that of Sir Andrew Macphail to write the history of the Canadian forces in the war can scarcely be

conceived." He insinuated that Macphail was a political hack who had been chosen to do a job and had
delivered. While some of Macphail's comments
echoed Bruce's own sentiments on the Babtie
Committee, the "official" history did have one advantage. The subject was interred for the next fifteen
years.

* * * * *

*The Provincial Legislature committee look into the
Medical Faculty and its relationship to teaching hospitals gave Bruce an opportunity to repeat previous performances. He stated that there was need of a top-
down re-organization and did not hesitate to criticize
the head and governing figures of the U of T. He was
able to speak with impunity as he had his own base
for operations and his own reputation of speaking out
fearlessly. Other witnesses had their own personal
axes. Although not all of his propositions were
enacted, enough were accepted to ensure his standing
in academia and as a result he would gain a chair on
the Board of Governors of the U of T at a later date.*

NOTE

Bruce's letters and comments are recorded in his book, *Politics
and the C.A.M.C.* (Briggs, 1915). Other comments by the Army
personnel are in the Perley Papers. The proceedings of the
Provincial Legislature committee are in the Bruce Papers,
Queen's University Archives.

CHAPTER 8

A Most Unusual Lieutenant-Governor

Politics make strangely led fellows. Perley, a graduate of Harvard and the son of a well-to-do lumber magnate, was following the banner of high office. After his war-time activities, he returned to the House of Commons and had been Secretary of State during Meighen's brief government. When R. B. Bennett swept to a Federal victory in 1930 with a resurgent Conservative party, Perley became minister without portfolio.

Bruce, the son of a dirt farmer, was following his "chiefest prize" — happiness. He had practised medicine with passion; fought his fight in the CAMC with verve; built a post-war life with affection, and married his chosen wife with adoration. He had been led by the thrill of living. Now at the age of 62, he was ready to settle his accounts and enjoy a life with his family. The two men, bound together by political ways, but split apart by bureaucratic means, still had something to give to their party and their country.

Perley, in his new office, was not a little surprised, and gratified, to receive a letter in 1930 from Bruce. Much time had passed, said the doctor; the situation in London had been tense, the War had been stressful, but now was the time to let by-gones be relegated. He closed with best wishes, to which Perley responded in a similar manner, saying that they should level the wall that had kept two Tory gladiators apart. It was appropriate; there was a stronger beat in Conservative hearts as Bennett took the reins of government.

It was fortuitous that the two had patched up their differences, as Bennett was searching for a Lieutenant-Governor of Ontario. The previous Honourable M. D. Ross had resigned, and although Chief Justice Mulock was substituting, the office was losing its lustre and there were ominous signs of anti-Imperialism and pro-socialism in the West. Bennett, Perley, King, and the Governor General all agreed that it was vital, in order to maintain stability, that the office be filled. The depression was turning the mind of the man on the street from pomp to provisions, and the trappings of an appointed, rubber-stamping King's representative were not to be afforded. A respected Lieutenant-Governor could counter destabilizing forces and help reduce the impact of poverty and unemployment. Bruce refused. He was at a crucial state of his medical career, having just resumed his active practice, and there was still a large investment in The Wellesley Hospital, which he hoped to recover. In addition, his farm and new house were demanding, and also he had some qualms about the necessity of the office.

But Bennett, acting through Perley, was convinced that there must be a Lieutenant-Governor, and that Bruce was the correct man for the job. In October 1932 Bennett wrote to Bruce saying he wished to visit on the 15th. When the day arrived Dr. Peter McGibbon, MP, came instead, saying he was an emissary from Bennett, who regretted that at the last minute he was unable to get away from Ottawa.

McGibbon passed on the word that Bennett was very anxious that Bruce should accept the Lieutenant-Governorship on the grounds of public service. He appealed to Bruce to make the same sacrifice as he had done during the War, because now the spread of communism in the West and the generally disturbed conditions throughout Canada, made the need for such a symbol more urgent than ever. McGibbon reasoned that unless a Lieutenant-Governor could be appointed who would command the respect of the people, Government House would no longer remain open and there would be a spin-off effect and provinces in the west might also close down the offices.

Bruce replied that he was deeply appreciative of the honour, but did not feel he could accept. However, McGibbon, wisely, said he would like to discuss it with Mrs. Bruce as well. He met with her and put his case. Four days later McGibbon received a letter of acceptance from Bruce. But Bruce insisted that he should be able to terminate the appointment at the end of the second year. He also mentioned that there had been agreement that the office would provide funding for reasonable entertainment. The terms of the contract were that Bruce would receive $10,000 from the federal government. The maintenance of the building was the responsibility of the province.

On November 1, 1932, Bruce embarked upon the most hectic, enjoyable, exciting, productive, quinquennium of his life.

It took barely eight weeks for him to warm up to his new career before he delivered his first speech, on New Year's Eve, 1932. It took at least five years before the full effect of his occupancy of the office was realized, after he retired.

Although the symbols of the young democracy included the visible ties to the Motherland, Lieutenant-Governors rarely spoke in other than homilies. They invariably were noble-looking, gracious, the embodiment of all the goods things that

accrue from living in a great democracy. Opening
buildings, presiding at meetings, reviewing troops,
delivering the Throne Address in the Legislature — all
of these were prescribed duties, which required the
incumbent to appear before the public. Of course
there were such things as giving the Royal Assent to
Bills that were put on his desk for perfunctory signing. Bruce accepted these duties but added an element that was unheard of. He actually became
involved in the politics of the country, avoiding direct
interference but acting as a lofty advisor who was
looking for justice, not votes.

During his years in office he spoke to meetings at
least every three weeks, in all giving more than 150
speeches. His wide-ranging subject matter included
the education of women, the responsibilities of the
teaching profession, youth and education, housewives, quacks and science, the importance of democracy, and many others. There were several principle
themes he developed, aside from the generalities,
which were demanded on being invited to a specific
meeting. On many occasions he chose to shock his
audience, frequently exposing that the emperor had
no clothes. On the 100th anniversary of the founding
of Toronto he fired a major salvo when he said, "I
refuse to confine myself to congratulations to Toronto
for its beautiful parks and the standards of its citizens." He then launched a blistering attack on the
city for countenancing the existence of the worst
slums in Canada. He stated the four-fifths of the
homes in the older parts of the city were structurally
unsound and presented deplorable medical conditions. He "... shocked the good burghers by making a
strong plea — in the name of prevention — to do
away with the slum dwellings in Toronto," wrote *The
Globe*. This speech was a prelude to at least 30 more

which were delivered in various parts of the province but generally within clear ear-shot of Toronto's politicians. The pressure he raised was so great that within eight days of his opening remarks, the mayor formed a committee to determine what to do and asked Bruce to be honorary chairman. Bruce enlivened his campaign by demonstrating to the newspapers the shocking state of affairs: he walked, with suitable photographers, through some of the worst areas unearthing the most sordid conditions.

Of course, no seated politician could be against cleanliness and good health, but some did raise the question of money. Calculations as to the cost of meeting Bruce's demands showed a back-breaking debt for the city. In addition, instead of tearing down and rebuilding, as Bruce suggested, there were counter-claims that the same objective could be attained with alterations. But Bruce, with a bit in his teeth, charged into the fray time and time again pointing out that nothing but a special tear-down, followed by a build-up of houses which had first-class sanitation would do. In the course of his proselytizing he brought out evidence from England, where a similar thrust was being made. Slum-clearance areas in the United States were also visited and the information gleaned was passed to the committee.

The level of his rhetoric was matched by his fact-finding. "Seventy percent of the 1332 dwellings which were inspected in the recent Toronto Housing survey, fell below the minimum health standards. Bad housing does not produce bad health alone. The influence of physical environment on crime and cases of mental breakdown is important." The newspapers picked up on his theme of "Our Blighted Areas" and *The Financial Post* launched a series on housing problems across the country, supplemented with stories culled from British publications, which reflected the same concern.

Bruce's strong advocacy caused some resistance. Controller George Ramsden exclaimed, "We should not put a noose around our people by taxing them twelve millions of dollars, just because the Lieutenant-Governor says so, until we know exactly what we are doing." He was voicing the general concern of elected officials with regard to cost. *Hush*, a scandal sheet, took advantage of the atmosphere to point out that the Anglican Church owned the dirty slums. "That clergy clearly bobble as property fall into ruin... why should the public redeem it." It claimed that rebuilding slums at public expense would be a gift to the rich Anglican Church. Sam McBride, who was elected mayor a few years later, urged that enforcement laws should compel owners of dwellings to install sanitary conveniences. "Before we go into a housing scheme we must see what houses can be made fit to live in and after this is done, we can decide when and how we would build homes."

Within a relatively short time the housing committee, chaired by Bruce, brought in a report which estimated approximately $12 million would be necessary to wipe out the slums in the city. It recommended that "...a serious and sustained public attack on the problem of bad housing in Toronto, by means of a modern and efficient system of town planning; a big response for repairing or demolishing unfit buildings and the building of new lost-cost buildings as rapidly as possible," was indicated.

Armed with the recommendations of Bruce's committee, Mayor Stewart approached Bennett for help with housing. The Prime Minister, who had expressed alarm to Bruce at an earlier date about the cost of the proceeding, immediately referred the request to a housing committee of the federal government. By August 20, 1935, the government had passed the *Dominion Housing Act* which called for investigation of housing conditions throughout the country and established the machinery for providing immediate financial assistance.

The Bruce Report, as it was now called, had been conceived in political apostasy, when the Lieutenant-Governer had challenged the city fathers, Bennett and King at the Centennial celebration. It was delivered with many birth pains as the country considered whether it was government's job to give this type of public assistance. It matured into a housing development — Regent Park — which was built 25 years later.

It was a masterful stroke when McGibbon, Perley's emissary from Ottawa, asked to speak to Angela after Bruce had refused the Lieutenant-Governorship. It was no secret that Bruce adored his wife and her every wish.

Although she had not been born to the purple, Angela readily assumed royal trappings. Chorley Park, the Lieutenant-Governor's official residence, offered a venue to be a real first-lady. Not for her the Eleanor Roosevelt presentation as a no-nonsense working woman. Now there was a place arranged for Angela to preside over the Royal Winter Fair, the Arcadian Court and to accompany Bruce to royal jubilees, military reviews, conferences and official duties under three consecutive kings of England. Bruce's bargain in his acceptance said that "...no elaborate program of entertainment would be required of me under existing conditions... ." The statement quickly buckled under the avalanche of visitors, the multiplicity of appearances and the burgeoning popularity of the silver-haired statesman and his beautiful consort. Bruce had to construct a support to wear inside his right glove for protection when shaking hands. Angela, from being a house-mother to a group of VADs, blossomed in fifteen years into an accomplished, admired chatelaine, who could supervise a household of many servants, solace her beloved Herbert in his adversities, and keep a diary.

Many dinner parties were noted in her book. Bennett was a regular guest with stories of W. L. M. King and his shortcomings. Massey, now the High-Commissioner in London, was declared to be a disaster.

Dr. Manion, who was Minister of Railways, and Bruce spent time discussing their old days in France. Manion, author of a book describing his experiences in a casualty station and his visits to a British Army hospital wrote, "...in the operating room some of the clumsiest of surgery was being carried on by a group of men who ought never have gone outside the sphere of medical work. ...stood silently watching this clumsy surgery being inflicted upon the helpless patients who came from the surrounding camps. It was really about the worst surgery imaginable, for these men had been practicing medicine — not surgery — in various parts of the world; and, apparently having been placed in charge of this hospital, they had come to the conclusion it was a great opportunity to learn surgery by practical experience (at the expense of the men in the army)."[1] This, of course, came as no surprise to Bruce.

Changing from the heroic mode to the distasteful was the constant stream of gossip and invective over Premier Mitchell Hepburn. His election promise had been to close Chorley Park and do away with the perfunctory post of Lieutenant-Governor. Angela recorded the stories of drunkenness, boorishness, and womanizing with appropriate disapproval. In particular she noted the recurring tales of warfare between Hepburn and King, but much more pressing was the imminent threat of closing the door of her domain.

Her anxiety and anger was assuaged by the visits of Lord and Lady Bessborough, the Governor General and his successor, John Buchan, Lord and Lady Tweedsmuir. Both of the latter were authors, which made for fascinating discussions and a budding friendship that was outside official politeness and terminated only with Buchan's death in 1940. Bessborough who in elegance of dress was matched by Bruce, established the Dominion Drama Festival, over which Bruce officiated on several occasions.

One of the most flamboyant visitors was Bruce's patron, Sir William Mulock. Although he had chosen the doctor at the turn of the century to be on the staff of the U of T, because of his outstanding surgical record, Mulock continued to be a powerful and kindly pater familias, ready to counsel or scold as needed. A custom established early in their relationship was attendance at his annual Christmas party, when Mulock, suitably fortified with cheer, would enter as Santa Claus and distribute gifts to all of his guests.

When not hosting a dinner, Mulock would take Bruce fishing, watering his rye whiskey from one side of the row-boat and being careful to pass urine on the other. Bruce was not an ardent fisherman but he enjoyed the time with his benefactor. Angela noted the honourable knight had an expert tobacco-juice ability to hit a spittoon, or a flaming log, when he was recounting some of his tales. At other times, when dining, she noted that he had two sets of dentures.

One was for talking and the other for chewing turkey, so when the fowl was in his mouth, the alternate plate rested mutely beside his dishes, waiting to enunciate. Even though Mulock dined frequently with Dean Primrose, it is not clear why he maintained his cordial relations with Bruce. Although he had supported his outspokenness during the war and appreciated his honesty at the time of the General reorganization, relations were strained when Bruce entered Federal politics as a Tory in 1940. Happily, good cheer was restored before the Grand Old Man of Canada died in 1944.

Bruce at 65 was beginning to outlive his friends, while Angela increased her circle. She was constantly in the newspapers and magazines through the many public functions she performed. "Mrs. Bruce wore a gown of beige lace with a chiffon flower on her shoulder, and her modish hat was beige." "Mrs. Herbert Bruce, smartly dressed in a coat adorned with rich-bound fox...wearing a lovely gown of cornish and purple satin, very simply cut, with flowers of the same material in front." It was not surprising that she was voted the best-dressed woman in the province. But there was substance beneath the satin, as she campaigned for funds to erect a home to train girls in domestic work. Bride Broder wrote in *The Star*, "Great benefit would accrue for this first aid assistance, unemployment would be lightened, the weight of anxiety and the daily struggle of parents to make both ends meet would be greatly helped." The previous year Angela had campaigned for money to start a training school for girls, and the following spring she offered to take an untrained girl onto the staff at Chorley to give a thorough training in cooking and household management. The times did not require that females should aspire to higher station.

Angela accompanied Bruce to England for the Jubilee Celebration and was invited to a series of social events with the Royal Family; she met the Duke and Duchess of Kent, the Duke of Devonshire, Mrs. Meyer Sassoon, Beverley Baxter, Lord and Lady Kemsley, and others. She diarized that it was an exhausting life, but she was enjoying it.

The Bruces attended the coronation of George VI as representatives of Ontario and were presented to the new monarch; they attended the military and naval reviews, and were in the official party, chaired by Leo Amery, which welcomed the Empire Youth Rally. It was all very exciting but concluded with a deflating return to Ontario politics.

A clash between the new premier and the high-riding surgeon was inevitable. Although there were many public photo-ops with Premier Mitchell Hepburn and Bruce shaking hands, behind head-lines, there was the dark threat of Hepburn's election platform. On the other hand, the two seemed to get along well together outside their official duties. Hepburn constantly explained that he was not adamant about closing Chorley, but was being pushed into that position by his cabinet. On several occasions he spoke frankly and told Bruce that the effort being made by Chorley was greatly appreciated and was a great benefit to the citizens of Ontario. This apparent amicability never surfaced in Angela's diary.

The guest list continued to contain the rich and famous. Lord and Lady Baden-Powell regaled the Bruces with the story of how the Scouting movement had begun during the siege of Mafeking. Yeats-Brown detailed how he had conceived the *Lives of a Bengal Lancer*, while standing on his head. He amused other dinner guests by demonstrating the position. John

Masefield, Poet Laureate, discussed the war poets, in particular, Wilfred Owen. Bruce mentioned that he had passed close to Owen's grave-site while searching for the grave of Lieutenant D. Cross, Second Bedfordshire Regiment, who had died of wounds on the 23rd of August 1918. Bruce was looking for the cemetery because Cross had been a close friend of Angela, before Bruce arrived on the scene. It is likely the two were engaged. The search, which began at the end of September, took several days before he could locate the actual site, and record it for Angela. Owen was killed on the 4th of November. One of the last things he wrote was, "Of this I am certain, you could not be visited by a band of friends half so fine as surround me here." He was 25.

Bruce was deeply empathetic for other young men who, in time of war, rallied to the colours but during the Depression suffered loss of dignity and vocation. This mindfulness extended to young women as well and at Guelph he lectured on the importance of the science of Home Economics and its service to the state. He urged that proper cooking and a balanced diet should be included in all courses in Home Economics, even suggesting that this was a compulsory qualification for marriage. For young males he warned that ".. in cities, deterioration both mentally and physically would occur with unemployment. It is not necessarily a mere training for a job which is required, but the kind of education which preserves sanity by broadening one's outlook." He planned in the new communities he espoused that there would be centres where classrooms and sports recreation buildings might go hand-in-hand. He had already observed this in Liverpool, England, and stated, "So clearly indeed do I feel there is a necessity for considered action by all communities for the alleviation of avoidable mental distress and physical degeneration, ...centers (could be established, which gave) a healthy invigorating community life that would benefit everybody." Health of the community was one of his major pre-occupations. Part of his rationale for better housing was to reduce the incidence of disease. Hand-in-hand with this went programs for the early recognition of tuberculosis, the immunization of infants, the establishment of convalescent hospitals, such as St. John's (which he opened), and a cancer hospital for London, Ontario. His proposal for new convalescent homes was made in order to avoid the "...present crowding of our hospital wards... partly due, I think, to the present condition of world affairs... this condition has made such movement imperative. Why, think of it — for space in nearly all our hospital public wards, at present there is a waiting list for 30–40 in almost every case."

In order to deliver medical care he praised, once again, the general practitioner. He pointed out in a speech on January 18, 1934, that the family doctor was dominant in the world of medicine and would remain so. He was the first who saw disease in all its phases while the specialist saw only the end. "There is a very real danger of narrowing down your interest. A qualification that doctors should possess, those of acute observation and acute deduction, tools which can operate in any field of activity, should not be confined within the narrow compass of any one person's specialization to the exclusion of all others."

Associated with the strong feelings about medical care were his reports of what he called quackery in any sense. On November 22, 1933, he claimed that serious depredations were made on health by fakes, and that the quack was a public enemy. "At a time when qualified, scientific doctors are equipped, as never before, to cope successfully with illness, disease and injury, quackery continues to flourish. Hard times for everyone else are boom times for quacks and charlatans," he advised. He charged that there was more money being made by quacks and vast, bare-faced, and unashamed corporations built on quackery, than ever before in the history of medicine. He then listed 100 types of "healing" and pointed out how women were victimized in numerous ways by the cult of beauty practice and the unending and increasingly bold frauds which were perpetrated upon them. For example, skin could not be fed by rubbing in creams. Eyelash and eyebrow dyes had been condemned in other countries but not in Canada.

He also supported A. R. Kaufman of Kitchener who was proposing birth control through the use of condoms and urged, religious beliefs to the contrary, that considerations should be given particularly where there were more children in the family than could possibly be considered healthy. Later in his term Bruce was especially critical of Charles Vance Miller, who had established a baby derby in his will. This curious document left shares in O'Keefe's brewery to protestant ministers and shares in the jockey club, if the legacy was accepted, to some holy fathers. The recipients would have to forego some of their principles.

However, in the most scandalous portion of his will, according to Bruce, Miller left a large sum of money, to be given to the woman who had given birth to the most children ten years after his death. "A poor biologic joke," was Bruce's comment.

A much happier note was struck when he served on the Jewish-Gentile relations committee beginning in April 1934. In association with Rabbis Jacob Hess and Eisendrath, he laid the cornerstone of Holy Blossom Temple and at that time attested to the magnificent tolerance that existed on either side. Addressing the Jewish-Gentile seminar on April 24th, he stressed that even in these times of anxiety, Jew and Gentile could take counsel together. After listing the great achievements by the Jewish community in the world, but particularly in Toronto and Ontario, he ended with "...the priceless heritage of tolerance, the precious gift of freedom which this city and this dominion, as part of a great Empire, hold in trust for this and future generations, will, I know, never be betrayed never be lost. For it is in this freedom, this tolerance, this true democracy that the richest life is to be found for all men." He expanded on these sentiments in his book, *Friendship: The Key to Peace*, published in 1937.

This book was a collection of speeches that he had delivered on various occasions, adding to the prior collection published in 1934, *Our Heritage and Other Addresses*. While there was occasional duplication in the published addresses most of them presented fresh ideas, different approaches, and novel suggestions on how the state of man could be improved. Friends, and enemies, wondered how he could maintain such a prodigious output. It is possible that he received help. Victor Ross, an old friend who had been the first to greet Bruce and his bride when they had returned to Canada, had been appointed Vice-President of Imperial Oil and was concerned largely with publications. His input was obvious, in some of Bruce's speeches. In addition, Frank Prendergast, a newspaper journalist, who was assistant to the President of Imperial, and had close contact with Hector Charlesworth of *Saturday Night*, was a constant visitor to Bruce's office and home.

These visits may have resulted in a letter, on government stationary, to a young Wally Prendergast, age 13, arranging an appointment for the Lieutenant-Governor of Ontario to visit the "Curio Museum" which Wally had in the basement of his parent's home. In due time, with proper pomp, the Kings' Representative in Ontario, and his consort, arrived at the Museum, presented a visitors' book, properly signed, to the young man, and congratulated him on his collection. In addition, they donated a number of WW1 artifacts, including a German helmet, and bayonet. The boy was flabbergasted and it took many years to determine how so high an official had heard of his project.

But there was more. From that time on the Prendergast children received Christmas presents every year from the Lieutenant-Governor.

But there were no gifts exchanged between Hepburn and Bruce. The Premier's platform to close Chorley appeared to weaken at times, only to be reinforced by his cabinet and by Hepburn's built-in vacillations. At the end of his first term, when he sought re-election, he had confided to Bruce that he had decided to drop the "Close Chorley" part of his campaign. However, when re-elected he returned to his original plan. Bruce pointed out that he was paid by the federal government; however, if the Ontario government closed Chorley and refused to pay expenses, Bruce would have no alternative but to resign. This threat checked Hepburn for a short time, but being a dyed-in-the-wool politician, he offered to make a deal. This involved King's appointment to the Senate of one of Hepburn's colleagues, who had been defeated in the election. If King agreed to this, then Hepburn would reduce his demands on Chorley. King, sensitive to a blackmail-type suggestion, which was a little beyond accepted political horse-trading, refused. In addition, he urged Bruce to stay on for a second term. But by this time Bruce had grown impatient with the continuous threatening atmosphere around Queen's Park and tendered his resignation.

When he left Chorley Park it remained empty; as the new appointee was housed in the Speaker's apartment at Queen's Park. Eventually, because a buyer could not be found, Chorley was dismantled, with pieces of the elegant building being sold off to one and all.

It was a memorable hour, said Sir William Mulock, in addressing a mass of banqueters who had gathered to congratulate the out-going Lieutenant-Governor on December 14, 1937.

> My desire and purpose rather is to appraise and articulate, if I may, the spiritual significance of an hour such as this. It may, I think, be justly assumed that, having regard to Dr. Bruce's public and professional labours, this must be one of the great hours of his career, for high above all other rewards associated with a man's life and his relation to his fellow-men must be the deep soul-gladness of that hour wherein those fellow-men conspire to do him honour and manifest in this laureate hour their gratitude, their confidence, their love.

And there was another plaudit. Bennett mailed a congratulatory letter. Bruce gave a gentle felicitation to Mulock. The response to the Prime Minister, cloaked in the required deference, fulminated.

> I am glad to learn that you think the duties of the office were satisfactorily discharged, in spite of the fact that you failed to give recognition for these services in a tangible way when you were in

a position to do so. Instead a painter of mediocre ability and a musician of undoubted merit in his profession, but whose inefficient administration of the Conservatory of Music as its director was causing much concern to the Board of Governors of the University.[3]

Bruce was furious that Bennett had left him off the New Year's Honours List and once again he had been refused the knighthood, which he deserved. He continued:

> I have fared very badly at the hands of Conservative Governments and not even a bitter political enemy could have received worse treatment that I from my party during the War. Andrew Mcphail was given a Knighthood.

Bennett presciently replied that he had no choice.

* * * * *

During Bruce's term as Lieutenant-Governor, Ontario went through a crippling economic depression. In 1933 more than 40,000 families were on relief assistance, with a food allowance of $4.22 a week. Many unemployed men took minimum-wage government jobs, leaving to go to the north for road repair and other public works. The pressure on the man in the street was overwhelming with frequent family break-ups, low birth rates, and an increasing growth of radicalism and communism. A march by several thousand men from British Columbia demanding jobs and other concessions from the federal government was stopped, with many casualties, in Regina, in 1935. But there was no evidence of this at Chorley Park. The Royal Agricultural Fair, The Horse Show, The Annual Motor

Show, The Queen's Plate at Woodbine, and other gala events went on with the vice-regal couple glamourously present in full regalia. Their son, Maxwell, went to Upper Canada College and, until he worked out a secret arrangement with the chauffeur, was driven in the government limousine. Peer pressure finally led to his walking the last few blocks to avoid the scornful remarks from his classmates.

Bruce never failed to shake the hand and have a word with anyone he met, whether at Chorley or on the streets of Cabbagetown. This sincerity and personableness contributed to his popularity and reflected postiviely on the office of the King's representative. During the uncertain days of the Depression, any symbol of stability was important. Bruce's stewardship was a contribution to peace and order, and his involvement in housing and health activities was a prelude to a new concept that government should become involved in social issues.

NOTES

1. Manion, R. J. *Life is an Adventure*. Ryerson Press, 1936: 162.
2. Bruce's speeches are all recorded in two of his books, *Our Heritage and Other Addresses*. Macmillan, 1934, and *Friendship: The Key to Peace*, 1937.
3. Letter, Bennett to Bruce, February 4, 1938; Letter, Bruce to Bennett, February 14, 1938. Queen's University Archives.

In his army uniform, with prematurely gray hair,
Bruce cut a smart figure.

As a young school-boy at Port Perry, then as a student at The University of Toronto and finally when he visited Berlin in 1902, he rarely smiled for his photographs.

*Bruce as a dashing ship's surgeon, enjoying himself in
Hong Kong with traditional Oriental clothes.*

*Bruce was Chairman or President of many organizations.
As President of the 1904 University of Toronto reunion
committee, he was a popular and efficient organizer.*

The palm room, a favourite spot with convalescents,
was turned into an eight bed ward.

By 1933, graduation day was a major social event under the elms.

The opening of the Wellesley Hospital by Sir Wilfred Laurier (left to right)
Dr. H. A. Bruce, Senator J. K. Kerr, Sir Edmund Osler, Dr. J. E. Elliott,
Lady Laurier, Mrs. R. J. MacMillan, Sir Wilfred Laurier, Dr. R. J. MacMillan,
Miss Powell, Dr. F. W. Marlow, Mrs. J. K. Kerr, Miss Elizabeth Flaws,
Sir William Mulock, Mr. A. E. Dyment (seated).

The original Wellesley, with the Bruce wing added.

The Stewart Bruce family in the 1890's.
Herbert stands between Robert and his father.

Bruce inspecting in the slums of Toronto prior to the Housing Committee Report. He rarely lost a photo op, particularly with young children.

Angela rarely rode, but cut a fine figure in the saddle.

The struggle over who would treat the cancer patients was obvious to the cartoonist who shows W. E. Gallie fighting with Gordon E. Richards over a piggy.

Whose Little Piggy Are You?

W E G

G E R

CANCER

TWAS THE MONTH BEFORE CHRISTMAS

Although Bruce was not "caricature" material, he was a cartoonist's target of opportunity. His stalwart stand against the baby bonus was a natural. His outburst against Brock Chisholm was good for a national laugh.

SANTA CLAUS BRUCE: "Oranges are short, so I'll just drop this rock in Dr. Chisholm's stocking. Hope it doesn't break his faith in Santa."

More Bedtime Stories

While Bruce was acting King of Ontario, his colleagues were fighting over the topic of cancer.

Always demure—but proud—the graduating class of 1915,
with Miss Flaws. The nurses prided their professionalism and were
the true strength of The Wellesley.

Dr. G. Murray demonstrates his artificial kidney at the opening of the
Caven Memorial Research Institute. From the left of Bruce, Dr. R. J.
MacMillan, Mr. Hugh McLaughlin, O.C., Dr. Murray, Lord Webb-Johnston.

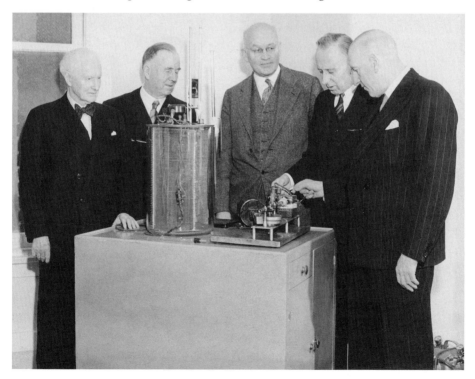

Maxwell and father on an outing.

Angela and Herbert on one of their frequent festive occasions, always just short of regal.

The family, out for a spin in the Packard touring car.

William P. Caven, a great friend of Bruce and supporter of The Wellesley.

A benefit from the union with the Toronto General was the
Elsie K. Jones nurses residence. In 1950 Bruce turned
the sod in company with student nurse Patricia James,
Miss Jones, Mayor H. McCallum and Board Chairman
N. Urquhart.

Angela continued her support of The Wellesley Hospital well after Herbert's death. She presents a cheque to Harold Turner, Chairman of the Board and Dr. Metro Ogryzlo head of the Rheumatic Disease Unit, for the Bruce Lectures. She clashed with Turner at a later date.

At the opening of The Wellesley Ross Tilley Burn Centre, Lieutenant-Governor John Aird backed by Premier William Davis and Ms. Joyce Bailey, administrator. Dr. John Provan stands behind Dr. R. Tilley.

The Wellesley became a 600 bed general hospital with a large nurses residence. The elms still shaded the front lawn.

CHAPTER 9

War Declared!! — on Cancer

There were those who said he should have stabled a white horse in his Bloor Street house, with which he could lead a current crusade.

In May of 1929, while addressing the Toronto Academy of Medicine, Bruce ignited a campaign to conquer an enemy that was killing more people than had died while he was Inspector General of the CAMC. The death rate from cancer was steadily on the increase. He quoted figures that showed in 1902 it was 54.8 per 100,000, which had risen to 69.6 in 1914, and by 1927 had gradually climbed to 99.6. With characteristic histrionics, he announced that soon 3,000 people per year would die in Ontario from this dread disease.

Certainly the cancer problem had been noted by others. Dr. W. H. B. Aikins, the son of Bruce's old professor, in 1915 highlighted the foreboding statistics. But it was not until an International Symposium on Cancer in New York, where figures were released by Frederick Hoffman, statistician of the Prudential Life Insurance Company, that the clear impact of the disease impressed the public.

Bruce, while attempting to dispel the pessimism surrounding the treatment of cancer, acknowledged that there had been a few encouraging developments, and several false hopes. The preceding year a Dr. Raymond Pearl of the Johns Hopkins had remarked that there was an incompatibility between cancer and

tuberculosis and therefore proposed injecting tuber-
culin into the cancerous tissues of inoperable cases.
The results of that trial were to be known some time
in the future. However, there had been disappointments. Professor Blair Bell of Liverpool had
announced at the Academy in Toronto some years
previously, a treatment with colloidal lead and stated
that he believed he had found a cure. This led to an
instant demand for the substance; however, a number of investigators reported that there was no evidence that there was absorption of neoplastic tissue
and the average duration of life in patients treated by
lead had been less than expected. In addition, there
had been severe toxic reactions, leading to anemia.

While acknowledging that surgery offered the only
chance for a cure when dealing with cancer in the
most accessible positions in the body, Bruce declared
that there seemed to be only one treatment for other
areas and it was radium.

The action of radium on cancerous tissue had been
mentioned in Canada during the first decade of the
century. Not only did it benefit some kinds of cancer
without the need for surgery, it could also be used as
a palliative agent. However, one of its major disad-
vantages was the cost. Realizing that this was a
major block to treatment, New York State had purchased 2.25 grams for $225,000, and made it avail-
able to practitioners.

Bruce saw this as the only effective means of treating epitheliomata of the skin, mouth, tongue, nasal
fossa, pharynx, vagina, and cervix. He said that it
had been used successfully in cancer of the rectum
and prostate. He, himself, had been implanting gold
seeds, which had been exposed to radiation, in a
number of patients and had achieved excellent

results with this material, which was not available to the general medical profession.

He then proposed that, following the example of the States and Sweden, a supply of radium should be purchased and kept in a central area such as the Physics Department of the University of Toronto, where radon seeds could be prepared. In view of the fact that a fund of nearly $4 million had recently been obtained for Industrial Research in the Province of Ontario, of which one half had been donated by citizens, he said that a similar sum could be raised to purchase radium. Patients who could afford to pay for its use would be required to do so, and those without means would be supplied free. He also urged that a "cancer hospital" should be established in Toronto for investigation and treatment, in line with similar hospitals in many cities in the United States, the British Isles, and Europe.

To provide a battlecry for his campaign, he said, "If a very poor country such as Sweden, with a population of six million, can afford 18 grams of radium... surely this very rich Province of Ontario with a population of more than half that of Sweden... should be able to afford half this amount."[1]

Bruce had had long experience with surgery for cancer. Before World War I he was doing two or three total mastectomies per week and he continued radical surgery in the twenties. This mutilation was always a source of discouragement to him, so he seized readily on the possibility that radium could be effective.

One of his chief allies was the Premier of the Province, Howard Ferguson. They had had many discussions of possible means of treatment, particularly after the British surgeon Lord Moynihan had visited Toronto to open the Banting Institute. He had been a house-guest of Bruce and they had discussed tactics. Ferguson, although interested, and feeling the pressure from his old friend, was faced with a disastrous financial situation in the province and was reluctant to advance the required capital. The Honourable Forbes Godfrey, Minister of Health in March of 1930, stated clearly that Ontario was not going to buy radium on the basis that "opinions vary as to its efficacy and this Government certainly is not going to invest any money in a supply at the present time."[2] To combat this parsimony, it was necessary to involve the public which was achieved by declaring a war. The rubric designed to recruit an army of supporters was that cancer cells were "Bolshevik cells" that had no obedience to the normal rules of cell growth and "corrupted" other cells. Thus the first shot heard around the province in the seven-decade "war on cancer" was fired.

As allies Bruce had a number of officials of the province including Dr. John McCullough, Chief Medical Officer of Health; Charles Hastings, Medical Officer of Toronto; and Dr. G. E. Richards, who was head of the X-ray Department at the Toronto General. Opposed to his propositions were two groups; the first were unfriendly and the second unthinkable.

In the first group were those physicians who disagreed that government should intervene any more in the health care. They had reluctantly given up the fight against government intrusion into the field of communicable disease prevention. Now they saw Bruce's scheme as a further expansion which would deprive the doctor of his rightful place in controlling disease — and collecting fees to do so. But this group had two internal problems. They could not agree among themselves who should be in charge of the radium. W. E. Gallie, of the University of Toronto, felt strongly that a surgeon should be the major instrument for the placing of radon. Others strongly agreed that this should be done by Richards or radiologists in a similar position. The second problem was that no one was really sure what caused cancer, so how could it be attacked?

Despite all the advances made by scientific medicine in the first 30 years of the century, there remained a mystery as to why cancer did occur. Dr. Madge Thurlow Macklin, who achieved great fame in the following years when discussing eugenic problems, published that tumours were more common in monozygous twins and that heredity played a role.[3] Hastings and others stressed chronic irritation in the development of cancer.[4]

Systemic causes were also blamed, which included a viral theory of cancer. Dr. W. Gye of the Imperial Cancer Research Fund suggested that these could be due to chronic irritation.[5] Frederick Banting visited Gye's laboratories in London and became interested in Gye's study of chicken sarcoma. Banting carried out a similar research for several years, which did not yield a positive outcome. The viral etiology followed closely on the bacterial theory, when it was abandoned.

These confusing and conflicting opinions, based usually on sound research by respected scientists, led only to haziness in the mind not only of the physician but also in the public. Hence the second group, according to Bruce — the unthinkables.

To Herbert Bruce, those who operated outside the mainstream of medicine — that is, without qualifications from a medical institution — were anathema. He spent much of his time exposing and contradicting their claims. He was industrious in pursuing the

variety of chemical agents which were prescribed,
such as arsenic, gold, benzine, calcium, and vita-
mins, to prevent tumour metabolism, but his major
concerns were with practitioners such as Hendry
Connell, John Hett, and Rene Caisse, who worked
outside of regular medical parameters. While he
understood that, because of the inadequacies of "scientific" medicine, sufferers might well look to other
sources for help, he had difficulty nevertheless in
understanding the process. "It is a sad mockery of
our vaunted civilization and an unanswerable indictment of our standards of education when it is possible for men and women of seeming intelligence by
their millions, to entrust their health and their very
lives indeed all that is most precious to them — to
those totally ignorant of the structure of the human
body, its normal physiological functions, and the
nature of diseases they profess to cure."[6]

In his zeal, he was tending to damn all efforts at
providing a cure. Dr. John Hett of Kitchener claimed
considerable success in treating the disease with a
serum which he had developed. Not only was it a
treatment but it could also diagnose the presence of
cancer. Patients suffering from cancers in all stages
but the final, showed a definite reaction to the inoculation, but there was no reaction to the serum if the
patient was not a cancer sufferer. He claimed that the
inoculation arrested the growth of malignant tissues
and thus was feasible to use in combination with
surgery, when the tumour could be removed either
before or after using the serum.

Hett had some credentials, for in 1904 he had
come into the province as an original investigator,
and was the first to treat uterine fibroids by X-ray.
He had studied in Europe for extensive periods, had
graduated from the U of T, and had served in several

political positions. He had run as a federal candidate on one occasion as an "Independent-conservative." Unfortunately, Hett would not reveal the make-up of his formula as he feared that it would be stolen by others.

Dr. Harris McPhedran was quoted in the newspapers on October 27, 1931, as saying "there are 10,000 of them" with a laugh, when told of the reported new cancer serum. "It is probably just some report that got out about him." He then challenged Hett to put "all his cards on the table for the medical profession to investigate." Hett refused and continued to advertise; he was eventually censured by the College of Physicians and Surgeons in 1937. However, he continued to see patients.

Hett's approach and zest for his treatment was similar to that of Dr. Thomas Glover of Toronto, who had attracted attention previously with the development of a bacterial serum for cancer. This effort, although popular for a short time, was eventually discredited.

Similar enthusiasm, which reflected the public's anguish at the failure of conventional medicine to produce results, gave the "ensol" treatment of Dr. Hendry Connell of Queen's University a boost. Although there was never a full assessment of his cure-rate, it remained popular for many years and received government support for investigation. When that research proved disappointing, the government transferred funding responsibility to the newly formed Ontario Cancer Treatment and Research Foundation (OCTRF).

Another controversial cure was right in the venue which Bruce enjoyed. Rene Caisse, a Bracebridge nurse, discovered an herbal remedy which attracted many sufferers and garnered a great deal of publicity.

She continued to dispense this potion, in spite of a great deal of opposition from the medical profession. She endured and before dying passed the formula for "essiac" to a private organization, Resperin. Even though it failed to pass the scrutiny of OCTRF Director K. J. R. Wightman in the post-war years, it continued to be supplied by another director, Dr. Matthew B. Dymond, a former Minister of Health for Ontario. Dymond, who had opposed the claims of the Hett serum, embraced essiac.

But all of that was in the future.

Bruce's friendship and favoured position with Ferguson was happily transferred to the new premier, George Henry, when Ferguson, who used Bruce as an intermediary, was appointed High Commissioner in London. Before leaving, Ferguson announced the government's support for a radium institute, and proposed that it would be at the Toronto General Hospital.

The momentum was picked up by Henry, possibly with some prodding from Saskatchewan, where a Cancer Commission had been established to work out a means to purchase radium. Henry appointed a Royal Commission on X-rays and Radium in the treatment of the sick in 1931. Contrary to the desires of the OMA, the Commission members were largely non-medical — John McLellan, Professor of Physics at the U of T; Walter Connell, Pathologist of Queen's University; Arthur Ford, Editor of the *London Free Press*; and John McCullough. The Commission was chaired by the Reverend Henry John Cody, currently President of the University of Toronto, and an old friend and confidante of Bruce. The friendship was temporal and spiritual, as Bruce occupied the front pew in Cody's St. Paul's Anglican Church.

Although the make-up of the Commission was criticized by the OMA initially, careful coddling by Cody and later by a newly appointed Minister of Health, Dr. James A. Faulkner of Belleville, managed to quell some of the objections.

Cody assured the physicians that their rights and privileges would not suffer by interference on the part of the government. After visiting many sites in Ontario, the Commission members went to Great Britain and Europe; in general repeated the findings that had been made by Bruce after an extended visit in 1930, when he had been able to persuade Ferguson to take up the cause.

The Commission recommended that there be established, in the existing hospitals, clinics and facilities for the use of radium, after the glowing reports they had received in Europe. The idea of the separate hospital was not supported, although Bruce offered The Wellesley as a possible site. This offer was not entirely altruistic as the hospital was continuing to lose money, and it was quite possible that Bruce was trying to marry his institution to a solvent spouse. Indeed The Wellesley had been a bridesmaid on several occasions, when attempts were made to join with the Grace and then St. Michael's Hospital. Both match-making efforts failed.

The result of the Commission's findings was that Ontario invested heavily in radium and made sure it was made available to a large number of physicians by establishing an emanation plant at the U of T for the production of radon.

When Faulkner took up his duties as Minister of Health, one of the first things that was requested was to investigate non-medically operated clinics that offered cures. This matter of "quacks" and "charlatans" was a constant focus of the OMA. The problem was addressed by The Wellesley Hospital Clinical

Society in 1937, which recommended that the government rule that all those centres claiming cancer cures, should submit their data to an outside body, which would evaluate the results. Bruce was obviously continuing his vendetta against non-medical healers. However, Faulkner, although he recommended to Premier Hepburn that he would become more strict with non-medical groups, failed to act decisively on many complaints. He was reluctant to prosecute Rene Caisse, who operated a clinic without a license and continued to do so for a number of years, and he did not discipline Hett.

By the late thirties the Canadian Cancer Society had begun to conduct educational and awareness programs; however, the coming of the second war with a reduction of manpower put most of the Cody Commission on hold, and it was not until 1943 that the new organization, the OCTRF was organized. By this mechanism the government downloaded its responsibility onto a not-for-profit, quasi-governmental organization.

Its mission was to diagnose, treat and conduct research in cancer. The make-up of the OCTRF Board ensured that a more conventional approach using current science and medicine would be used.

Bruce continued his watchdog efforts over non-qualified practitioners but by the end of the thirties had taken on other causes. Although Chorley Park was only a deserted memory, the Bruce aura still hung over Ontario politics. His pleas for "Our heritage — tolerance," continued to motivate Christians and Jews to live in peace together. *The Kingston Whig-Standard* on December 13, 1934, wrote "..in exquisite language he tells of the priceless heritage of tolerance and the precious gift of freedom which the Dominion holds... ."

That same gift of language, the elegant phraseology, plus a sense of the theatrical made it possible for him to persuade his audience of the correctness of other non-conformist ideas.

The championing by a respected leader of a birth control message in another campaign, while shocking to some, was gradually accepted as the road to a reasoned planning of families — and a vital step forward for the rights of women.

There was also the political hagiology that he, a Tory Lieutenant-Governor, had refused to authorize a $500,000 payment to the Dominion Construction Company, which was presented as an Order-in-Council by a Tory Premier, George Henry, who had just been defeated in election. It was a singular act of incorruptibility, which was a beacon in a political world with its plethora of paybacks, bribery, and shady contracting.

The account was eventually presented again, after editing and negotiation by Hepburn, and paid. This independence on the part of the the Lieutenant-Governor may have established some connections with Hepburn, who frequently crossed party lines, particularly with King. The Prime Minister insisted that the St. Lawrence Waterway was in Federal jurisdiction, while the Premier claimed that part which was within Ontario's border. There ensued a running feud between the two, which eventually catapulted Bruce into the spotlight of the Federal Government.

Prior to that, there was the matter of Chorley Park. Hepburn's platform, which appealed to unemployed, frequently desperate Ontarians in the middle of the Depression, was to cut civil service, sell off government cars, and get rid of the expense of the Lieutenant-Governor. On being elected, the Premier refused to be sworn into office by Bruce, but eventually had to give over. Next, he ordered that no Liberal was to attend social functions at Chorley, and set the example by never dining at Government House. A standard piece of any of his speeches was to deride the office, but in private he got along well with Bruce. This was a tribute to Bruce, who neither drank, nor smoked, nor "womanized." Mitch was notorious in each of these three arenas of behaviour, which were outrageous to a staunch Anglican. But that same Anglican had a touch of envy for the way the Premier, in his prime, was handling the social problems of the province, although that changed later when Hepburn lost his ability to discipline his life and deteriorated.

The Wellesley again began to recover its potential. Bruce continued his surgical activities and the hospital was fully occupied when the Lieutenant-Governorship ended. In addition, Bruce appeared before the Committee of the Provincial Legislature to consider whether practitioners such as osteopaths, chiropractors, naturopaths, and others, should be permitted to use the title "Doctor." While agreeing that the medical profession did not forbid differences of opinion, Bruce insisted that disputants must have a knowledge of basic facts, before they could enter the discussion. As far back as 1911 Bruce had reported to the OMA that he had considered the training schedule for osteopathic schools in the United States and concluded that it was practically worthless. In 1920, he headed a committee of the Academy of Medicine to investigate the claims of a practitioner who maintained he had a serum for cancer, which was shown to be false.

Bruce made a strong declaration before the committee which eventually ruled that these practitioners were not allowed to style themselves "Doctor." While leaving the committee rooms, Bruce was man-handled by a group of drugless practitioners, who were furious over his testimony. Eventually, the Attorney General of Ontario made a public apology for what had happened. In spite of his small stature, Bruce had a wiry strength and was able to take considerable buffeting. He was prepared for his next challenge.

"I had some experience with Mr. Bull during the war and I am very reluctant to have anything to do with the matter at all," stated Bruce on August 13, 1938, at the inquest into the death of Mrs. Maybelle Sidley. Twenty years after he had uncovered Bull's sham convalescent centre in Putney, the two men were thrown together by the court.

Mrs. Sidley had died under suspicious circumstances in Bull's Rosedale home. The inquest attracted fashionably dressed women, eminent counsel of U.S. and Canada, most of the Faculty of Medicine of the U of T, and a horde of the curious. She was the daughter of the Horlick Malted Milk Company owner, an American multi-millionaire, William Horlick. He met and was impressed by the resplendent Canadian lawyer-entrepreneur Bull during a trans-Atlantic crossing and invited him to stay as a houseguest near Chicago, Illinois. It happened that Maybelle was having difficulty in securing a divorce from her husband Dr. John Sidley. By hiring detectives, Bull was able to conclude the divorce action, earning Maybelle's gratitude, but Sidley's hatred. The surveillance led to a lawsuit which eventually paid off with a settlement to the husband. In the interim the stock market crashed and a penniless Bull stayed on at the Horlick house, even after William Horlick died.

While recovering his finances, Bull had to make a hurried exit from Chicago. According to some reports,

Sidley, seeking more revenge, hired a gangster to terminate the Canadian lawyer. While fleeing, Bull's car crashed and he had to continue to Windsor and then to Toronto with two broken legs and a lacerated forehead, in an ambulance. He recovered and by now, a widower, set up his home, Loren Hall, in Rosedale, where he entertained lavishly, and became known as the Duke of Rosedale.

In 1934 Maybelle arrived at Loren Hall, expecting, hopefully, to become a bride, but was downgraded to a paying guest. She remained over the years and by 1937 was showing some signs of mental deterioration: she would go daily to the Union Station to meet her son Bill, whom she said was coming from Chicago. He never arrived.

Her health was a concern to Bull and he requested a consultation with Dr. Ray Farquharson, professor of medicine. At the inquest he stated that she had a neurological condition which made breathing difficult and, as he was leaving for the west, he asked Dr. Trevor Owen to handle the case. Owen reported that on June 17, 1938, she was unable to hold a pencil because of her weakness, and asked for further consultation with Doctors Ian Macdonald and Robert Armour.

Word reached William Sidley that Maybelle was desperately ill and he became suspicious that there might be foul play, as Bull was allegedly the main beneficiary of her $4 million estate. Sidley contacted Dr. Smirle Lawson, Coroner for Ontario, on July 4th, and asked that he and Dr. Herbert Bruce examine the patient to determine the cause of her illness. His suspicion that something was out-of-joint was heightened by a chauffeur's comment that there were iron bars on her windows.

Meanwhile Trevor Owen had made a diagnosis of

amytrophic lateral sclerosis, a disease of the spinal column which affects walking and breathing. Sidley arranged for an eminent neurologist from the Presbyterian Hospital in Chicago to examine the patient but Macdonald refused to have another consultation. Bruce on 5th of July asked Farquharson if he and Lawson could examine the patient but Farquharson refused. This refusal was tempered by late afternoon when the lawyer for the Sidley family persuaded Farquharson to permit the consultation. Lawson and Bruce arrived at the patient's home at 6:00 pm that evening and waited until 8:00, but they were not allowed to see the patient, because "she was too sick." Maybelle Sidley died the next day at 8:00 am.

All the ingredients for a newspaper frenzy were present. There was the notorious, wealthy, bachelor lawyer. There was a millionaire heiress who lived in the same house and had had a "...mysterious illness over several months." One paper reported that she was "taking a large bottle of bromo seltzer daily!" There was a team of renowned University professors, which had refused to permit equally famous medical figures to examine the patient. There was the possibility that the only son of the deceased had hired a civil servant, the Chief Coroner of Ontario, to perform an examination. And there was the death's-door arrival of the Chicago neurologist who was refused permission to enter the patient's room.

The account at the inquest by the various physicians who had taken care of Maybelle was straightforward; however, an autopsy had not been performed, so it was difficult to be sure of the cause of death.

Bruce admitted, under cross-questioning at the inquest, that he "...thought there was some suspicion that she was being restrained as a prisoner in the house." He also admitted under close questioning, that there were "...some suspicious circumstances connected with her case; that is, that her death might be due perhaps in some measure to something else, rather than natural causes."

The nub of the contention was that the cause of death was uncertain and that Farquharson had refused to allow an autopsy.

Putting all these factors together Attorney General Conant of Ontario ordered an autopsy. At the same time Bull was subpoenaed and his bank accounts frozen to insure that any proceeds from the will could not be moved and that tax would be collected. There was a flurry of investigations of Mrs. Sidley's financial affairs and in particular a systematic check-up of all bank accounts in the name of Bull, to determine what money had been passed from Mrs. Sidley to himself. It was alleged there had been a transfer of $1.5 million over a period of a few years. No succession duties had been paid on this amount.

Eventually an autopsy was performed. Dr. E. A. Linell confirmed that death was due to widespread involvement of the nervous system, amytrophic lateral sclerosis. Dr. Joslyn Rogers, after extensive testing, stated that there was no poisonous material found to account for death.

Bull received $250,000 from the estate with the rest going to Maybelle's son and relatives and some surprising amounts to churches in Toronto. Bruce lost an old friend, because he felt that Dalton McCarthy, Bull's lawyer, had been too aggressive in his cross-examination and had cast aspersions on the Bruce name.

* * * * *

It was surprising and disappointing that Cody did not recommend that the government should accept Bruce's offer of The Wellesley as a cancer hospital. The tour that the Commission made in Europe showed the clear advantage of a hospital devoted to the diagnosis and treatment of cancer, but local medical pressure and politics led to cancer care moving into the general medical stream, where it competed with other specialties for beds, funding, and research money. It took another twenty years for the government to realize the effectiveness of a dedicated facility. The Princess Margaret Hospital, which became Canada's showpiece for cancer care, opened on vacant land immediately beside The Wellesley, and the two hospitals shared staff and research for many years.

NOTES

1. Bruce, H. A. "An address on the treatment of cancer." *CMAJ*, May 1929: 475.
2. *Toronto Star*, March 18, 1930.
3. Macklin, M. T. "Tumours in monozygous and dizygous twins." *CMAJ*, 44: 606.
4. Hastings, C. J. Health Bulletin. May 18, 1927.
5. Gye, W. "The Causation of Cancer." *CJMS* 58 (1927): 58-59.
6. Bruce, H. A. "Address to the Kiwanis Club." *CLP*. May 1934: 145.

CHAPTER 10

The Garbage Pail of Europe

"The deformed should not reproduce, and I don't care if sterilization or birth control is used to prevent them." Dr. W. E. Gallie, Professor of Surgery at the University of Toronto, a bear-sized man who growled forcefully on all subjects, did not hesitate to speak his mind on a matter that was generating public anguish and academic heat across Canada. The professor realized that it was a harsh judgment he delivered while addressing the 1930 Ninth Conference of the International Society for Crippled Children in Toronto. His decision sent a shock wave through hundreds of health workers and parents who had come to hear the foremost straightener of bent limbs and teacher of the growing number of orthopedic surgeons, who would treat dislocated hips, spinal deformities, club feet and a myriad of other problems that were seen daily in nurseries across the country. Gallie, who had pioneered the use of tendon transplants, was a force in University circles and his opinions were respected throughout the world.

His declaration raised a storm of objections all over North America, but his ideas were supported by an eminent scientist in genetics at the U of T, John W. MacArthur. Each of these knew that they would stand in the eye of a hurricane, but were determined that the words had to be said. In truth the reasoning did not differ from those of the "Father" of genetics, Darwin's nephew, Francis Galton, who at the annual

Huxley Lecture in London 30 years previously, in 1901, had called for the segregation and sterilization of the "undesirables" — the feeble minded, the insane, the deformed, and the epileptic. This presentation was heard by Bruce, a colleague of Gallie, while studying in the U. K., and stored away for future reference.

The early years of the 20th century marked the zenith of Victorian liberalism. Social problems could be met and solved by a harmony of science and religion inspired by Christian virtues. The previous century had read Darwin's thesis on the evolution of species extrapolated by the authors such as Cesare Lombroso, who had published that "bad blood" determined criminality. Science, embodied in Herbert Spencer, author of a renowned book, *The Principles of Biology*, and Galton had said that certainty could be found by a new breed of scholars who could predict the outcome of human unions, as surely as a breeder of livestock could raise the quality of his herd by culling poor stock. By the end of the century, the findings of the researchers justified each person's place on the social ladder, because, if like begat like, there was little that any intervention could be expected to do. The poor, the imbecile, the maimed, and the sick, would always be with us. Galton stressed in his speech his desire that the number of people born with "genetic" disorders could be reduced and that the physically fit would have more children, which would lead to an improvement in the race.

When Darwin and Alfred Russell Wallace had preached their gospel, in the 1860's, the major opposition had been the church, but now, a half century later, other defenders sprang to the bulwarks to protect the ability of a doomed human to change, to be elevated, to take a rightful place in society. It was possible to break the straight jacket of germ plasma postulated by August Weissman, which dictated the shape and content of progeny to come. The social sciences, rather than chemistry, botany, geology anatomy, and other hard disciplines, had flourished and flowered; anthropology, social work, and psychology were now capturing the eyes and ears of the public and parliament. Franz Boas, world-acclaimed social anthropologist, had completed his field research with convincing evidence that man was "shackled by culture." Heredity played only a minor role. His students, Ruth Benedict and Margaret Mead, joined in the crusade against the forces of biological determinism.

The confrontation was not an academic exercise. Canada, Ontario, Toronto, were staggering under the incubus of a massive immigration. Some observers said that the nation was becoming the "...garbage pail of Europe." "We don't want a nation of organ grinders and banana sellers in this country," shouted MP E. N. Lewis during debates in the House of Commons.[1] However, the musicians and fruit peddlers were not the real threat. Criminals, imbeciles, and paupers with inherent defects were. In a lecture at the Toronto Orthopedic Hospital, at the corner of Bloor and Yonge, Charles K. Clarke, Professor of Psychiatry, discussed the aetiology of mental disease. While acknowledging that physical changes in the brain cortex were not fully understood, he said that "...the symptoms of a disease are apt to be greatly influenced and exaggerated by the morbid hereditary basis, which underlies so many forms of mental disease." He had no doubt that heredity played a major role in the production of defectives and the insane, illustrating this by describing two persons of different strains brought up in exactly the same environment, subject to the same training. When they matured they had little in common. This difference was due to a morbid constitutional basis, and not to the environment. A further example were post-mortem changes associated with Korsakoff syndrome, a type of memory-loss disease, supporting his thesis that all mental disorder had an organic basis and the greatest cause of them all was heredity.

Clarke determined that trauma, as a cause of mental disease was rare, and, quoting his findings in the records of the Franco-Prussian War, showed that only 60 persons became insane among the many thousands who had sustained head injuries.

His was not a lone voice shouting in academia. Other U of T men were equally convinced that Canada was committing "race suicide" by admitting "...a large number of those who have, no doubt, been such as is well calculated to breed degenerates." as pronounced by the Medical Officer of Health for Toronto, Dr. Charles Hastings.[2] Dr. J. G. Adami of McGill University declared to a meeting of the Canadian Medical Association in 1912 that it was a "...puerile view that it is a perfectly sound policy to welcome as citizens, those of degraded or depraved parentage."[3] Adami, U of T Professor Ramsay Wright, and Sir William Osler had chaired the First International Eugenics Congress in London in 1912, presided over by Leonard Darwin, the son of Charles Darwin, with Vice-President Winston Churchill and Alexander Graham Bell, who had made a plea for the deaf to refrain from marrying.[4] There was a rising wave of evidence throughout the western world, that abnormalities were heritable and that it was incumbent upon countries to maintain their borders against disease-carrying immigrants.

This message was not well received by many of the new sciences, which, following in the footsteps of Boas, argued that the body was born with a clean slate and nurture wrote the scenario of life. Part of this philosophy stemmed from the ideas of Sigmund Freud who theorized that many mental problems arose in childhood and resulted from guilt associated with one's sexuality. His message had been current in Canada, since his disciple, Robert Jones, had practised in Toronto. Jones and Campbell Myers of the General made strong cases that there was not an inevitability to insanity and therefore treatment could cure many disorders. In the Annual Report of the General for 1907, Jones claimed cure results in cases with pronounced cyclical symptoms. He reported from the Out-Patient clinic in 1909 that he could find no clear evidence that mental symptoms were more common in eastern Europeans, contrary to other researchers, and that "...it was possible to do a considerable amount of good, more than my personal wish could have anticipated."

These differences of opinion over the causes and treatment of disorders made interesting dinner conversations at the General or at faculty meetings. While Bruce cared for some of the orthopedic conditions that resulted from "tainted blood," he did not press his opinions regarding hereditary disease. He was, however, an adamant proponent for an Anglo-Saxon Canada, a member of the British Empire, and he applauded Clarke's efforts to restrict and select immigrants. This philosophy had popular support as it built on ethnic prejudice. But these efforts were overwhelmed by the Federal government's aggressive immigration policy. Even the passage of the *Immigration Act* of 1910, which prohibited entrance of idiots, imbeciles, feeble-minded, insane, and epileptics, was ineffective because of the shortage of doctor inspectors.

The inability of the government to answer the concerns of many professionals reflected some of the uncertainties which faced policy makers. Was there a direct relationship between the parents and mental and physical diseases, and especially the mentally feeble, or criminal and immoral groups? Were the behaviourists justified in their claims, which downplayed biological inheritance and stressed cultural and environmental factors? Or was there a pox on both these medical camps who were contesting dominion over thousands of citizens. Perhaps health was dependent on the Victorian virtue of clean water and soap? Besides, it was accepted that each village had someone who was "slow."

This heated argument was put on the back burner in 1914 with the outbreak of WW1. Immigration ceased and the emphasis was transformed from who entered the country, to what should be done with those defectives, already landed. Bruce, a classmate of Gallie, had first-hand experience of the general state of well-being of Canadians from his wartime observation of the high number of recruits for the British and Canadian Army who were rejected as unfit. During the last stage of the war, the figure reached almost 40 per cent. In addition, only one in twenty candidates for the Toronto police force met desired standards. He applauded the publication of Dr. Helen MacMurchy, who graduated from Toronto in 1901 and then worked in the obstetrics and gynecology department of the General. During that time she became aware of the appallingly high infant mortality rate, almost 20 per cent of all deliveries. Her concern and advocacy resulted in her appointment as medical inspector of schools and then as inspector of the feeble-minded in Canada. To her thinking it was paramount that the mentally challenged should be identified and in some cases segregated, as it was common knowledge that they were the basis for pauperism and criminalism. Her annual report on the extent of the problem culminated in a book, *The Almosts: A Study of the Feeble-Minded* (1920), which alerted all Canadians to the sub-normals. Its message was that money spent on educating this unfortunate group to avoid the evils of illegitimacy, venereal disease, prostitution, and crime, was wasted, and that to protect society it was necessary to institutionalize.

MacMurchy's conclusions were not unique. In Nova Scotia, a League for the Care and Protection of the Feeble-Minded; in Manitoba a series of articles by J. S. Woodsworth (later founder of the CCF party); an MA thesis by McMaster University student Tommy Douglas on "Christian Sociology," and the Canadian National Council for Combating Venereal Disease, directed by Dr. Gordon Bates, all added weight to the urgency of this problem. Bates wrote that VD and mental deficiency went together. The Council's mission mandated that the feeble-minded should be watched, as C. K. Clarke in a report in 1917 recommended, with public registration for the disease and segregation of the deficient. Although the government did not wish to go so far, in some areas there was a widespread opinion that the only solution was sterilization.

In the first ten years of Canada's Century the major concern had been the flood of immigrants, with suspect deficiencies. In the second, although the tide of defectives from outside had subsided, compulsory schooling, and later intelligence testing, revealed an unsuspected, unrecognized sea of feeble-minded.

During the third decade attention again turned to the ocean of immigrants pouring through gates which had been re-opened by the government. This inundation was driven by the profit to be made by the railroads, shipping companies, and landowners as the prairies were colonized. Public figures such as Charlotte Whitton of Ottawa protested against the dumping of surplus labour into Canada, but had little effect on the government of Mr. King. Nor did medical opinion have any leverage. Clarke announced that of 125 immigrant girls seen in his clinic at the General, 67 were deficient, 36 were prostitutes, 31 suffered from venereal disease, and 18 had illegitimate children,[5] although efforts had been made to conduct thorough pre-embarkation examinations. The Canadian Medical Association in 1927 warned against an influx of inferior immigrants who produced large families, but it was not until 1930 that a newly elected Conservative government closed the gap.[6] It was ironic that in truth, it was the Depression and not the legislation, that dried up the flood, which did not resume until after WW2.

Gallie's declaration to the Crippled Children's Society marked a refocusing by the medical fraternity on the issue of what should be recommended with the mass of immigrants, and others, which had been landed in Canada and were threatening to outnumber, and outvote, the Anglo-Saxon founders of the country. It was crystal clear to any Canadian that the foreigners were the source of many social problems. And to any interested person, there was overwhelming evidence of the increasing number of feeble-minded. The Rockefeller Foundation in funding a mental diseases unit at Toronto and McGill, provided a base for increasing the number of psychologists, including W. E. Blatz and E. H. Bott. This augmenta-

tion in expertise insured that there would be a burgeoning stream of reports, which would inevitably
identify more sub-normals, as testing programs
became more sophisticated. Each published paper
indicated more research to be done, but no research
examined the cultural bias of the tests.

Bruce could relate to this looming crisis with all his
being. While he was not an expert in mental diseases
and feeble-mindedness, he was keenly aware of a
threat to his beloved Canada. He could echo the
keening sentiments that many of Canada's future
hopes had died at Vimy, Passchendale, or Gallipoli.
He had known and had been with John Macrae. He
had spent evenings with Yellowlees in the Academy of
Medicine before that brave colleague had died in the
Bosporus. And there were many others. And now, as
Lieutenant-Governor, he was going to be able to contribute to preserving his country.

The change in emphasis from erecting barriers to
identifying the foreign elements that were already
present granted an opportunity to work with the
newly formed Eugenics Society of Canada in 1931.
There was much to be done, because Alberta, and
shortly after British Columbia, would have
Sterilization Bills. Each required permission of the
parent, which presumed that an informed decision
could be made. But both Ontario and Quebec, the
two largest provinces, were unconvinced of the advis-
ability of similar legislation in view of the resistance
of the Roman Catholic Church, which had objected to
sterilization from the first. The two western provinces
had few Catholics.

In one of his early addresses, Bruce laid out his
concept of his function:

> On many occasions and at various functions a
> Lieutenant-Governor is expected to speak.

Speech-making is a privilege — a duty insepara-
ble from his office.7

Bruce was taking a few liberties. Yes, previous
Lieutenant-Governors had spoken on many occasions about the King and Empire, and Canada's
future. Never had a royal appointee sounded off on
current matters. Bruce, with his track-record of
doing it in his own way without going through normal channels, set a precedent, not only for Ontario,
but also for Canada and all areas where a Crown
appointee officiated. He stopped just short of involvement in the politics of the country — leaving that to
Chris Patten — but influenced much of the political
process of the province.

Bruce brought more than facts or eloquent
speeches to elevate the debate in the arena. His royal
presence added respectability to the arguments. No
other Canadian of such prominence spoke out. And
such a flow of rhetoric — a mixture of hyperbole and
perceived truth. Sterilization was "...damning up the
foul stream of degeneracy and devaluation, which are
pouring pollution into the nation's lifeblood." To some
members who attended the 40th annual dinner of the
Canadian Club in Hamilton on April 20, 1933, such
brazen championship, delivered after the usual congratulatory homilies by the invited speaker, may have
been an anti-peristaltic. Bruce explained that his
advice was given at a time of "...one of the most terri-
fying of these natural problems. It is race degeneration... if the present rate of increase in mental cases
continues for the next three quarters of the century,
half of the population of the U.S. would be in the
insane asylum..." He quoted from Henry Martin
Robinson's book, *Insanity: The Modern Menace*. To
palatize his talk, it was necessary to disarm his audience of any suspicion of special pleading by a medical

man. He did this by quoting an old Hebrew maxim: "Do not dwell in that city whose Governor is a physician." After an appropriate response, he could move on to the remainder of his menu:

Elizabeth Tuthill, a woman of splendid qualities, lived nearly 200 years ago in Hartford, Connecticut. She married Richard E. Edwards, a great lawyer. They had one son and four daughters. That union left its mark upon American blood.

Later in life the same Richard Edwards married an ordinary, common-place woman. She had ordinary, common-place children. This splendid heredity of Richard Evans was swamped by the mating. But the union of the two streams of fine blood of similar character begets greater. The son of the first marriage was Timothy Edwards, one of the founders of Yale University. He was the father of Jonathan Edwards who married a wonderful woman, Sarah Pierpont. From that union have descended twelve college presidents, 265 college graduates, 65 college professors, 60 physicians, 100 clergymen, 75 army officers, 60 prominent authors, 100 lawyers, 30 judges, 80 public officers, state governors, city mayors and state officials, 3 congressmen, 2 United States senators, and 1 Vice-President of the United States.

Nor is that all. Direct descendants of this Jonathan Edwards included: Aaron Burr, who was Vice-President; Mrs. Eli Whitney, wife of the inventor of the cotton gin and the novelist, Winston Churchill.

He continued to speak of the lineage descendent from Elizabeth Tuthill which included Grover

Cleveland, Ulysses S. Grant, and the widow of Theodore Roosevelt.

He then described the descendants of Max Jukes who had also lived in New England 200 years previously.

> The melancholy story of the descendants of this degenerate can now be told: 1220 of these social scourges had been traced. Of the descendants of Max Jukes, 300 died in infancy, 310 were professional paupers, 440 were wrecked by disease, 50 were prostitutes, 60 were thieves, 7 were murderers, 53 were criminals of some other kind, many were habitual drunkards addicted to every form of vice and depravity.

Bruce was quoting the Tuthill and Jukes cases from a study published by Robert L. Dugdale in 1874, who was convinced that the results of his inquiry established a clear genetic basis to crime.

Now was the time to drive home the pragmatic point of his speech:

> At present Ontario spends $4 million annually to maintain hospitals for the insane. But the "Max Jukes" of this province go their way un-checked and un-restrained. "like begets like", and so they propagate their kind at a rate, which requires that every 20 months a new asylum be built at a cost of $2 million and with an annual maintenance charge of $ 300,000.
>
> In the mental hospital in Orillia there were several groups of half-a-dozen from the same family. You can in imagination trace the course of such un-checked propagation. The seeds of deficiency are transmitted from generation to generation, continuously affecting an increasing number of unfortunates and imposing upon the shoulders

of the mentally and physically fit a heavier bur-
den, which, by its economic weight, discourages
them from raising large families.

Between 1871 and 1931 the Ontario population little more than doubled but the number of
insane in our institutions multiplied six-fold and
the cost of caring for them increased ten-fold.

...The remedy, the recourse which can save us
from the horrors incidental to a continued spread
of deficiency, is sterilization for individuals con-
templating marriage when there exists the taint
of insanity, mental deficiency or epilepsy in the
family....Sterilization of the unfit is not open to
objection on the ground that it comprehends race
suicide. On the contrary, it is the antithesis of
race suicide; for what could be more suicidal,
what more destructive to any race to permit
degeneracy to increase at its present pace? It is
indeed suicidal for a race a nation or a province
to cast its germ cells, its precious jewels of heredity, into the oblivious, bottomless sea of mental,
moral and physical degradation.

It was a speech designed to recruit not doctors, but
businessmen, community leaders, and eventually
government to the cause.

A follow-up exhortation at the Academy of Medicine
in Toronto the next month used similar figures and
examples, with a greater emphasis on the medical
aspects. Present in the audience were Sir William
Mulock and University of Toronto President Canon
Cody. "I am not a technician with words" self-effaced
the speaker, "...but there is an influence that may
stultify future efforts of our profession and which
even now is working against all progress". He
continued:

It is a problem of racial degeneration, manifest

in mental and physical defects, symptomatic of a disease which is slowly and surely eating its ways into the heart of the nation. It is a disease whose victims multiply with a alarming rapidity, and its spread can be counter-acted only by state action. Today we are spectators of a phenomenon that has brought prouder races than ours to ruin.

To the medical man, as to all right-thinking men, life is a sacred thing. Our profession is devoted to the preservation of life; and religion and moral sense revolt to the suggestion that we can take life into our own hands. But surely there can be no religious or moral scruples against preventing propagation by the unfit. There can be no religious or moral principles which will sanction a reversion to savagery, and that is the road any nation will go if there are no restriction to prevent the sub-normal and the unfit from over-running the land.

Bruce did not add anything new to the discussions. His Hamilton speech was reported in the *Canadian Medical Association Journal*[8] with a strong endorsement by the editor, A. J. Nichols, and his assistant, Dr. A. G. MacDermott. They were joined by R. C. M. Hincks, C. B. Farrar and William Hutton of the Canadian Eugenics Society, and Dr. Madge Macklin of the University of Western Ontario. Each warned wholeheartedly of the fecundity of the feeble, promoted in part by medical advances. It was only just and fitting, since part of the dilemma had been fostered by medicine, that a medical solution — sterilization — should be provided. Indeed, the balance of sub-normals to normals was being tilted even further to disaster by the fact the normals were now practising contraception. (This practice was scorned by

MacMurchy, who accused housewives of preferring to play bridge and smoke rather than do their duties as mothers.)

Farrar, a psychiatrist, added more impetus to the movement. He viewed crime as a sickness. "The average criminal, being also a mental invalid, gravitates most naturally into a life of habitual crime. It is not only somewhat absurd, but often specifically dangerous, to allow such individuals to be at large at all." He continued to argue the hereditability of feeblemindedness, hence criminality, and that sterilization recommended itself on economic grounds, particularly if the family was, " ... of inferior stock, who must constantly depend on charity, and with whom birth control technique is impractical."[10] Support for neutering appeared from other prominent Ontarians. Agnes MacPhail, the first woman to become a Member of Parliament, told the United Farm Women, "I just wonder how much longer we are going to allow sub-normal people to produce their kind. You farmers, would you want the worst type of your cattle to be seed bearers?"[11] Bruce's prize herd of Ayrshires was a high-profile answer to that question, as was his yearly attendance and opening of the Royal Agricultural Fair and the Horse Show in Toronto. Blood lines accounted for everything.

The comparison to good animal breeding carried a great weight of conviction as mayors and reeves of Newmarket, Belleville, Brantford, Sault Ste. Marie, and many other smaller towns joined in sending resolutions to the Ontario Government to enact the appropriate legislation. Bruce pointed out that Ontario should be on the same path as twenty-seven American states, but Hepburn still did not act. In part this may have been a by-product of the armed truce that existed between himself and the

Lieutenant-Governor. Even when approached by Bruce, Rabbi Eisendrath, and Hutton, the Premier said only that he was continuing to gather information. Other examples and reports filled Ontario and Canadian newspapers. The *CMAJ* featured an article by MacDermott, which lauded the California sterilization experience.[12] *The Canadian Doctor* in 1936 published an item that described and defended Germany's sterilization program. A great amount of money had been saved from the "erasure" of reproductive powers in over 200,000 people. The author claimed that this procedure had resulted in decreased taxation. Bruce, who had visited Germany, recounted his experience:

> Already 50,000 idiots have been sterilized in Germany. What does that mean? It means that there are 50,000 mental defectives in Germany whose bodily functions differ not at all from their normal fellow-countrymen and women but henceforth they will be unable to have idiot children.[13]

With the rising volume and intensity of such public discussion, there was pressure on the Canadian Broadcasting Company to present some of the pros and cons. Although the Corporation had denied access to proponents of either birth control or sterilization, it changed its policy in 1938 and asked the Eugenics Society to arrange a series of broadcasts. Bruce was selected to give two sessions on the Nazi sterilization policy. This contribution was sandwiched between Hutton's accustomed zealotry and an anthropologist, C. W. N. Hart of U of T, who gave a standard low-key talk on Evolution 101. Bruce pulled out all the stops. He praised the Germans' astuteness in sterilizing "...300,000 useless, harmless and hopeless people." Not only was the Nazi action in harmony with nature: "It reinforces in the human species that selective urge which prevails throughout the rest of nature." It could even be described as merciful. He finished his paean with the declaration that Canada needed the same "biological housecleaning."[14]

It was generally acknowledged amidst the clouds of self-congratulations in eugenic circles that Hepburn must now take action. He did. He appointed a Royal Commission on the Operation of the *Mental Health Act*, which agreed that sterilization was indicated on certain grounds. But the Government failed to act on the recommendation, refusing to follow the lead of other non-Catholic provinces.

Beyond the ultramontane considerations, there was a growing opposition to the whole approach to the solution of the increase in the feeble-minded, the jail-prone immigrants, and the amoral indigent. The answer was in the numbers. They simply did not add up. In January 1937, a colleague of Bruce in the School of Hygiene in Toronto, Dr. A. H. Sellers, authored an article in the *Canadian Journal of Public Health*[15] that exploded the "myth" that the number of feeble-minded was on the increase. This followed a revisionist article in *The Canadian Doctor*[16], which lamented the non-critical enthusiasm in many physicians whose fervor rather than facts was misleading the public. Bruce himself was criticized as having little sound knowledge of genetics, particularly in view of the fact that the current finding of recessive characteristics gave new dimensions to "like begets like." Even MacArthur, who had sprung to Gallie's defence seven years previously, accused Hutton of creating panic in the name of Eugenics.[17]

The cracks in the structure built by sterilization were premonitory to the collapse of the edifice. In a remarkably short time the western world forced itself to look at the sterilization program in Germany, which had been endorsed in the mid-thirties, but now was seen as a sinister device which had been transformed into extermination for political reasons. Eugenics became synonymous with the brutal genocide practised by the Nazis and was no longer acceptable.

* * * * *

Bruce, and the others who were so adamant about the necessity of sterilizing some citizens, never publicly recanted. He did not live to read the earth-shattering discovery of genes and the possibilities of predicting diseases, or their prevention by gene manipulation. But he continued to have a strong conviction of the residence in the body of certain criminal traits when he wrote to Mr. Justice J. C. McRuer, who headed the Royal Commission on Sexual Psychopaths in 1957:

The urge to commit these crimes arises in the testicles. The only way to prevent them is to remove these organs. Even assuming for the sake of argument that the psychiatrists are right in their opinion that these criminals should be confined in a mental institution (which I do not believe) this operation which renders them impotent should be done before their release, for the protection of our women and young girls.

NOTES

1. Debates, House of Commons. 3: 3-4.
2. *CJMS* 21: 73.
3. *CMAJ* 2 (1912): 980.
4. *Nature* 89 (1912): 558.
5. *Canada's Child Immigrants*. Ottawa: SSCC, 1924.
6. *CMAJ* 17: 1927: 349.
7. Bruce, H. A. *Our Heritage and Other Addresses*. MacMillan, 1934.
8. *CMAJ* 29 (1933): 260.
9. *PHJ* 17 (1933): 83-89.
10. Sterilization and Mental Hygiene, *PHJ*, 22: (1936): 93.
11. *Toronto Mail*. December 4, 1935.
12. *Toronto Star*. February 17, 1936: 1.
13. Bruce, H. A. Address to the Toronto Conference on Social Welfare, April 24, 1936.
14. The Future of Our Race; series of radio addresses, n.p. 1938, Eugenics Society of Canada: 21, 22, 23.
15. *CJPH* 28 (1937): 132.
16. *CD* August 20, 1936: 30-34.
17. *SW* 1937: 15.

Other quotations are from Bruce Papers, Queen's University Archives.

CHAPTER 11

Back to the Trenches

No one was surprised when Bruce, in September of 1939, was refused by the Canadian Army, after volunteering his services. Maxwell, his son, was commissioned in the Royal Canadian Artillery, but father was seventy-five. Age meant little to the surgeon, who was still able to do the usual appendectomy in six minutes. His disappointment was made more frustrating when he observed that King was making very little preparation for the conflict, because of the "phony war". This listless pace was shattered and Bruce was thrust into conflict by his old adversary, Hepburn, who rammed a motion through the Ontario Legislature on January 17,1940, which regretted that King "...had made so little effort to prosecute Canada's duty in the war...." George Drew, the Conservative leader in Ontario, supported the motion, which, even though the Liberals held a strong majority in the federal House, King took it to be a vote of confidence, and he called an election. Bruce was outraged. He claimed it was quite unnecessary and was simply a political move to prevent any debate in the House about Canada's role until after the vote.

Bruce in the past had considered running for political office, after the Babtie Committee Report, but had never stood for election. Now, with his increased public stature, five Conservative ridings in Toronto were anxious to recruit him, and finally, after pressure from Manion, he allowed his name to be put up in Parkdale. It was a wise choice and he had a 1115 majority, requiring him and Angela to commute to Ottawa when Parliament was in session.

The Liberals took 127 seats and the Progressive Conservatives increased their number to 68. Bruce sat in the front row of the Opposition with Earl Rowe and rookie John Diefenbaker. Each shared the other's faith in the Conservative platform, but Bruce was more urgent in his desire to avoid the manpower problem of WW1 by bringing in a conscription bill as soon as possible. He saw this as a prime necessity in order to make a major effort in France. His maiden speech was on May 28th, eighteen days after Leo Amery in the British House of Commons, London had thundered to Chamberlain, Cromwell's famous tirade, "You have sat too long for any good you have been doing. Depart, I say, and let us have done with you. In the name of God, go!" Bruce looked across the floor of the House at King, "...a very lonely man," and commenced his speech with remembrance of his past friendship and admiration of the Prime Minister, "He is a man of high character, a man of peace."[1] But those were not the qualities to lead the country in time of war and forced Bruce to suggest that King should retire and turn the leadership over to J. L. Ralston, the new Minister of Defence. Such presumption from a neophyte member was unheard of.

"Mr. King was very angry and, I think, never forgave me," Bruce ingenuously commented. There would be more occasions for the surgeon-statesman to raise the ire of the Prime Minister in the future, as the Opposition continued to press for a greater war effort.

On December 7, 1941, the Japanese entered the war with their attack on Pearl Harbour; three weeks later Hong Kong fell, and with it 1900 men of the Winnipeg Grenadiers. There was widespread criticism of the Government and the Defence Department; an inquiry was called, chaired by Sir Lyman Duff, which exonerated the Government of any specific blame. Drew, now Premier of Ontario, challenged the Duff report findings with specifics, which showed clearly that a fiasco had occurred. Bruce was in the House to press Drew's charges.

"Dr. H. A. Bruce was the storm centre of today's resumed House debate when he urged that the public demand there should be a free debate of the Hong Kong affair," reported *The Globe and Mail*. "Dr. Bruce was repeatedly called to order by the Chair," continued the article, as it outlined his attempts to enter Drew's remarks into the Parliamentary record and, at the same time, to comment on the failure of the King Government to enact conscription. The main thrust of his argument was that, "There is growing indignation among the people of Canada over the government's hysterical efforts to stifle full parliamentary discussion of the Hong Kong expedition." He then read from evidence quoted in the Duff report, but stopped short of the final sentence, prompting the following response from the Minister of Defence:

Mr. Ralston:	Read the next sentence.
Mr. Bruce:	I will read it. It says "In these circumstances no finding can be made upon them."
Mr. Ralston:	In other words, what the honourable member read, is for effect.
Mr. Bruce:	I just stopped for a moment to get my breath. I had underlined in red pencil to read.
Mr. Ralston:	The honourable member took a long breath.

This interplay was ended when Bruce characterized the failure to include the statement of one of the witnesses as "reprehensible." This prompted the Speaker to request that Bruce withdraw the term as un-parliamentary. Bruce did so reluctantly and after suitable protest, substituted "incorrect." The Speaker ruled that that word, should also be withdrawn and Bruce finally gave in with, "It is not real debate we are having, it is a contortion and travesty on words to call this a debate."

The heat of Bruce's speech was fanned by the fact that the Justice Minister had suggested that Drew should not have used certain statements as they gave comfort to the enemy as to other details of the lack of firepower and accoutrement shortcomings of the Hong Kong force. But as the Report was six months after the surrender, it was in order for Drew to reply that the Japanese were already aware of those factors.

The debate in the House was cooling down when a Liberal member stated that Drew had impeded the program of the Bren gun manufacture. This immediately cued another rebuttal from Bruce who defended Drew, stating that he had been the foremost to advise and initiate the manufacturer of the Bren in Canada, and adding that the availability of those weapons in Hong Kong could have made a great difference.

Ralston and Bruce tangled at a later date when the news of the terrible defeat at Dieppe became public. Bruce charged that the Lieutenant-Colonel directing the operation should have realized the desperation of the situation and drawn back. Ralston argued that by throwing in reinforcements the tactical objectives could be achieved. Neither proponent could triumph, given the number of casualties and prisoners.

Bruce was enthusiastic in his opposition role. He

maintained an increasing series of criticism of the Liberal majority. "Confidence is lacking in our present government," he told a Kiwanis meeting. He continued, "Party government in war time is like facing your enemy with a horse and buggy instead of a cannon." He could have advocated tanks, as he did in May 1940 when he urged that Canada should immediately start to manufacture tanks. But C. D. Howe, Minister of Supply, derided this suggestion. However the Minister changed his mind, or saw the Bruce light, because two years later he proudly announced and showed pictures of Made in Canada tanks.

The same response followed Bruce's argument that Canada should act as a base for training Air Force personnel. This idea was turned down by King, only to be reversed later, with the founding of the largest training scheme for pilots, navigators, ground crew and other personnel in the British Commonwealth Air Training program. Bruce, who had heard from Vincent Massey, Canadian High Commissioner in London, lost no time in revealing that the program did not include provision for Canadian airmen to be under Canadian leaders, but were to be members of the RAF. This was a reprise of the arguments during WW1 about who should command Canadian troops.

Although the main preoccupation of the House was the war, there were other issues that claimed Bruce's attention. He prepared a Private Member's Bill on the Order paper in 1940, but it had not been brought forward by 1942. On the other hand Bills for divorces, up to 100 per session, had taken up valuable time, to which Bruce strongly objected. He felt that divorces should not be considered in the federal House. Neither Quebec nor Prince Edward Island wanted divorces handled in their provincial courts, so they had sent them to be processed in Ottawa.

He continued his focus on health issues which had been one of his chief thrusts since the 1920's, and was appointed to a Select Committee to study details of Health Insurance and Social Security chaired by Ian Mackenzie, Minister of National Health and Welfare. This proposal, which had come forth in the Throne Speech in the spring of 1943, was to examine social insurance legislation of the Dominion and other countries and to work out practical measures for Canada, including health insurance. There were 21 members of the Committee and Bruce shared responsibilities with fellow conservatives Diefenbaker, R. Adams, G. E. L. Mckinnon, and R. H. McGregor. Bruce was the most active in the group, with almost constant attendance, while the others appeared only sporadically. There were many long discussions and expert witnesses were called, with representations being made by many groups who were anxious to partake of any government money that might flow.

Mackenzie began the proceedings by outlining the principles of Britain's Beveridge Report, so-called womb-to-tomb, which had been proposed to guarantee that nothing would prevent good health in the U.K. One of the major contentions in Canada centred around how such a scheme would be funded. Many Federal members were conscious of the possible expense of an overall insurance scheme. Facts presented by the Canadian Hospital Association showed that in 1935 the cost of illness in Canada was $240 million. From this it was estimated that the total cost of an insurance program would work out to $20.45 per capita per annum, or 50 cents per week. However, adjustments were to be made for large families and other special circumstances. Bruce was strongly in favour of a contributory element for any type of payment; he insisted that total public funding would be deleterious to the system. However, he was able to promise that good health could be planned by a combination of public health measures and education, and recalled his speeches given during the housing debates in Ontario, which stressed the importance of youth health programs. By March 30, 1944, he was able to have the Committee adopt his resolution that there would be partial contributory funds. He was adamant that there should not be state medicine but rather there should be health insurance.

One of the stumbling blocks that the Committee faced was some reluctance of the Canadian Medical Association to come on board. Estimates showed that only 28 per cent of Canadian physicians would agree to the program. Bruce made it his personal business to meet with the organization. "I met medical men and I think the reason that a certain opposition has emerged from the doctors to this measure of Health Insurance is that they don't understand it," he reported. Doctors were just too busy to get more than a general understanding, he claimed, and after he had spent a few minutes discussing the measures with them at the annual meeting, the general comment was, "Well, I guess it's all right." This increased the number of physicians who would accept the scheme to well over 70 per cent.

Bruce's advocacy of the health insurance was extended to radio broadcasts on the CBC and the National Farm Radio Forum, and he made numerous presentations to medical and other related groups. Although it was pointed out that poverty and lack of sufficient money prevented some families from getting medical care, Bruce disagreed that Family Allowance would solve the problem. It was agreed by the Committee in general that the Family Allowance issue, which had been raised previously, "...has been a dead one since the Parliamentary Committee of 1929 turned it down."

Bruce also faced some old foes when the chiropractors and osteopaths made a strong bid to be accepted as potential recipients of fees from the system. As before, he was able to argue against their inclusion, although many members of the Committee were in favour. This position applied particularly to the application by the Christian Scientists for inclusion. Bruce objected strongly for any consideration on the basis that Christian Science was a cult and not, as claimed, a healing profession. He had done intensive investigation of the works of Mary Baker Eddy, "...the thrice married, once divorced author" of the book *Christian Science and Health*, which was the basic philosophy of the sect. In addition, he had been in touch with Dr. Morris Fishbein of the American Medical Association and collected a great deal of material which exposed, in his mind, the charlatanry of the "science." However, Bruce ran into a strong opposition with Mr. J. W. Fulton, the representative of the Christian Science Committee on publications, who sneered that Bruce had a closed mind and did not understand how Christian Science worked. Fulton published several letters that swayed public opinion. Bruce countered by quoting from Mrs. Eddy's instructions on healing and concluded, "I submit this is neither a prayer nor an invocation but an incantation, reminiscent of the days of witchcraft." He then modified his statement to the effect that even if it was a prayer, as Fulton had suggested, why should the Christian Scientist be paid, when the clergy did it for free.

He bolstered his argument with citations from several courts in the U.S. and specific instances of judgments that had been given against the Christian Scientists for withholding proper treatment from the sick. But, Fulton was not finished and made a strong statement to the Committee, which by now was tiring of this constant back and forth argument, and voted that any further discussions would be held in camera. Bruce insisted that he should be allowed to reply to Fulton's last statement, in front of the public with media present. After considerable argument the Committee agreed to Bruce's making one final public statement. The issue ended with the opinion that the irregular healing group should not be paid from a government funded Health Insurance program.

With the adoption of the Bill by the Committee, prior to going before the House for vote and enactment, the *Canadian Hospital* rejoiced:

> One great benefit that will appear in this proposal is that the day of hospital deficits and hospital grants will come to an end. Every patient will be a paying patient and the problems of municipalities will no longer have to make good the cost of indigents and non-paying patients.[2]

An exhilarated Bruce, who felt that he had been a major contributor to the decisions, entered the House prepared to vote for the proposal. However, not all the Conservative members agreed with the implementation of the Bill. Meighen had written to Bruce on the January 13, 1944, that there were many obstacles. Bruce replied:

> While I am aware of the many difficulties in putting such a measure into practice, particularly in a sparsely settled country like Canada, I believe that the time has come when it is necessary to insure that every human being when ill, will receive proper medical care whether they can

pay for it or not. This is the one form of social security that I favour, while believing that the Beveridge scheme is altogether too Utopian.

The draft of the Health Insurance Bill to cover all Canadians was the result of two years of intensive study. Bruce was convinced it was an excellent proposal; however, many years would pass before it was brought in.

King, and his cabinet, chose to bring in the *Family Allowance Act* on July 24, 1944, instead of presenting the Health Insurance Bill. This was a shocker to Bruce and others who had been kept in the dark by Ian Mackenzie, and had assumed, as had been agreed previously, that Family Allowance was not on the table.

The stage was set for the greatest Bruce brouhaha. He rose in the House and stated, "This measure is a bribe in the most brazen character made chiefly to one province and paid for by the taxes of the rest." He accused King and the Liberal Party of pandering to Quebec, which would receive the largest Allowance payments, while the other provinces in Canada would foot most of the bill. The Liberal members of the Committee were astounded at such a forthright stand, and Mackenzie asked Bruce to withdraw his statement. Bruce refused.

> I think it is going a long way to stretch the rules of the House. I have always been willing to abide by the rules of the House. I make no reflections on any member of the House. They're entitled to vote as their conscience dictates. I regarded this measure as a bribe and still regard it as a bribe. I have said so and I will not retract that statement.[4]

The Speaker of the House, acting as Committee

chairman, declared that the honourable member had made a statement which reflected on all honourable members who had supported the motion. He once again asked Bruce to withdraw.

Bruce replied, "I have already said that I made no reflection and intend to make no reflection on any honourable member." Bruce maintained that he had made that statement against only the measure and he had a perfect right to make it.

The Speaker of the House then took his chair; he received the Report of the Committee and placed it to the vote. It passed.

The Speaker then returned to the Bruce matter, asking the honourable member once again if he would withdraw his remark. Bruce refused. The Speaker then asked Bruce to withdraw from the Chamber until the House decided what it would do. As it so happened this was just prior to the dinner interval. There was little food for King, the Speaker, and members of Cabinet, and it was reported by *The Telegram* that the "Deputy Speaker was thumbing through the rules book."

Eventually some regulation was found because when the House reconvened, the Speaker ruled that Bruce be suspended from the sitting "...for uttering unparliamentary remarks."

> When the history of this time comes to be written, as histories of such times as this do get written at last by others than tame biographers retained for the purpose, lo, the name of Herbert Bruce, MP, is going to have quite a lead on the rest of the 1944 Canadian Parliamentary guide.
>
> For the honourable member for Parkdale has proved himself a Parliament man in the old and honourable tradition. And the scene his lone defence of Parliamentary freedom produced in

the Canadian House of Commons on Monday was a scene for the books if ever one was. Not a cheering scene; the betrayal of its own rights by a Parliament that has forgotten its duty; but one that history can use.

Judith Robinson of *The News* ended her account of Bruce's suspension by reporting that it lasted for two and a half hours.[5]

The Telegram reported: "Mr. King would doubtless feel that he saved the dignity of Parliament by refusing to allow the word bribe to be whispered within its sacred precincts. The public, it must be suspected, would find it rather difficult to understand why so astute a politician as he, allowed a disturbance of this kind to so thoroughly underline the charge which Dr. Bruce made."

Bruce, aware of the press and public reaction, re-entered the Chamber through the main door the next morning. He arrived in the middle of a speech by King. There was a burst of applause, which forced King to stop for a moment. Bruce marched up the centre of the House, bowed to the Speaker and then to the Prime Minister, before taking his seat on the front bench of the Opposition.

The national press comments continued from *The Globe and Mail*,

Moral courage is an infinitely rarer quality than physical courage. Dr. Herbert A. Bruce has shown that he possesses both these qualities in full measure. ...during a forced absence from the Chamber last weekend, Dr. Bruce was the object of a boorish attack by the Prime Minister. His offence was that he dared to stand by his convictions and condemned the Family Allowance Bill as a measure primarily to win votes for the Liberal party in Quebec... King had sneered at

Bruce as belonging to a past era. His attacks were vigorously applauded by the Honourable Ian Mackenzie and other sycophants, who, on their records, are not worthy to un-loose the latchet of the Parkdale member's boots.

Dr. Bruce knew from past experience he would have to face the hostile mob of the government majority. He had been hooted down by the solid Liberal phalanx before. He alone had stood forward to insist that Canada could and should build tanks while the Minister of Munitions Howe, stubbornly held that this was impossible. He had suffered taunts and abuse to force the Minister of Defence to disclose information as to the reinforcement situation of the army, and to express the views of his constituents on the Government's mobilization policy.[6]

In all his career Bruce had never received so many commendations. Letters of congratulation came from all levels of the public. The comments ranged from "Your speech on Family Allowance drew blood" to "You were the victim of a stupid ruling by the Speaker, who is a Liberal partisan." "Congratulations on your stand... the rest of the party lost face in voting for the measure." "Congratulations on your stand on the baby bonus."

Poems such as "Diaper Dole" by A. N. Other eulogized Bruce with,

Someone's sure to have a headache
when they start to call the role
of the near 4 million children
on the country's diaper dole.

Other comments were slightly earthier.

He has the guts, I'll say he has

although his hair is white,
he showed it in the last great war
and, yes, he still can fight.

Dr. Charlotte Whitton, C.B.E., of Ottawa wrote in
The Globe and Mail,[7] "...a review of existing systems
raises a serious challenge to any contention that the
system of cash grants for children has been long or
generally established or proved."

Possibly the most incisive comment was made in
The Ottawa Journal when it wondered whether
Parliament was becoming too "sissy." It reviewed
many of the famous shafts that had been hurled in
the past, such as a description of Peel,

> " 'He has a smile like the gleam of a silver plate on
> a coffin.' They have never been afraid of strong
> words in the Mother of Parliaments. Perhaps it is
> because they realized that anger is among the
> cleanest of the passions, and that indignation, even
> if expressed in heat, or perhaps cruel language, at
> least indicates devotion to a conviction which is not
> a bad thing."[8]

The inability of the Federal Conservatives to challenge successfully the King Liberals was a pervasive
pre-occupation during Bruce's political life. Part of
this emotion was fired by political ambitions, and
part by a personal disdain for the Prime Minister. In
1940, when explaining his reason for running in
Parkdale, Bruce said "...Why after a busy life, in part
devoted to public service could, should at this date I
offer myself as a potential candidate, in times so
arduous for public men? My answer is that no personal sacrifice can be too great when directed
towards such a cause as the freedom of mankind,
and the preservation of the Empire which has contributed so much towards the establishment of that

freedom ...share too the resentment felt by many of all shades of opinion that Prime Minister Mackenzie King is stabbing in the back responsible government." He further demonized King by stating that he was "...too much of the school of Hitler himself."

There had been high hopes with Meighen, which lowered precipitately with his inability to attract voters, particularly in Quebec. His old friend Manion was never able to fill the ballot boxes. John Bracken, who entered the Federal field with all the credentials of a successful 20 years as Premier of Manitoba, was not covering himself with glory, in spite of the fact that the Conservatives had now pre-fixed themselves with "Progressive".

Bruce was, once again, seeking to find a new Moses who could lead the party to the Holy Land.

On December 20, 1946 he wrote a letter to Beaverbrook:

> Many of us believed that George Drew would make an ideal leader as he has a splendid appearance, was one of the best speakers in Canada and has proven himself a capable administrator by his handling of the affairs of this Province. However I need not tell you how difficult it is to change a leader when I recall when it was in your House during the last war, that you assisted in getting rid of Asquith. Many people in our party believed that it would be disastrous to make a change at this time and it will have to go ahead with Bracken for the next election. After all the people will vote to get rid of King rather than elect our party. To do this we think they are more likely to turn to us instead of the CCF's.

His admiration for Premier Drew was based on a record of being able to work together. When Drew announced his twenty-two point platform in July

1943, Bruce was delighted. "If you cannot win, then I despair of the intelligence of the citizens of Ontario," he wrote. The pair were involved in the following spring when Ralston was to announce a plan to pay military doctors $ 4000 a year to work in rural areas. It was proposed that the provincial government pay the salary and collect the income. This was an incursion into health matters, clearly a provincial responsibility, without consulting Drew. Bruce raised his objections in the House and the problem of servicing rural areas remained unsolved, but he was able to make a strong plea for a Dominion-Provincial Conference to address health issues.

At that time Bruce had received word from Meighen of a presentation by a Dr. Eid of Macklin, Saskatchewan, who made a "... presentation, authenticated as it is by authority, is a masterly and devastating indictment of Health Insurance... ." He apologized to Meighen that he disagreed in this matter and five days later in addressing the residents of his riding, he repeated his position. He said that he would give his support "... to any enactment which, in my judgment, will bring this about, but reserving the right to challenge any detail which I think can be improved"[3]. He continued that "The implementation of Health Insurance in Canada requires grave care and judicious application by the State, the people and profession. It isn't something that can be turned loose; it will be a question of trial and error."

All of this talk was in anticipation that the Health Insurance Bill, of which he had been one of the architects, would be brought before the House in the near future. He promised that there would be provided medical, surgical, obstetrical, and dental care, drugs, hospitalization, and nursing. He estimated that the Dominion would offer the provinces eight different grants, and that the plan would cost $250 million a year, half obtained by contributions, half by taxes.

While outlining the curative portion of the proposed Bill, he emphasized that there would be a full functioning of preventative measures that would result in more permanent results. "Our hope for the future is bound up in prevention rather than cure."

He enthused over the recent "...milestone in the evolution of hospital care," when it was announced that Drew's Ontario government proposed to underwrite general hospital care for the entire province. In addition he lauded the planned campaigns against tuberculosis and venereal disease and indicated that the Ontario government "...has no intention of waiting for a Dominion Health Legislation." All of these plans were to be carried out against a renewed interest in housing conditions, with a revival of the Bruce Report on housing, given ten years previously.

> Although my report was shelved without action being taken, I am glad to see that there is at last a revival of interest in this subject and perhaps a serious attempt will now be made to provide decent houses for those in low income groups. In my opinion the provision of good housing for our people is an essential part of any health measure.

Bruce had further opportunities to repeat his ideas. On June 11, 1945, another election was called. Bruce had not intended to renew his candidacy, but he explained later that he "...was urged to do so by both Mr. Bracken and Colonel Drew for, otherwise, it was feared the seat would be lost. So here I am again, but will not find it necessary to work quite as hard owing to the valuable transfusions of new blood into our party." This was an "official explanation" to an

admirer writing from the West.[10] However on April 24,
1945 he had written to Maxwell,

"Now I have to make an explanation for having
gone back on my word, when I promised you I
would not again stand for Parliament. I hope you
will consider that under the circumstances I really
had no alternative. I tried my best with the assistance of John B. and other influentials here to have
the Executive Committee of my riding adapt George
Hees as our candidate. This they refused to do and
seemed indignant at such a suggestion being
made. ...the Executive and other members of the
organization, including John, urged me, in the
interest of the party generally, to accept the nomination and contest the riding in the expectation
that I would be able to carry it. At this time every
seat in the House is of great importance."

In the campaign Bruce made extensive use of radio
addresses. On May 26th he outlined why the Liberals
had brought in the Family Allowance Bill.

For some years... there had been a demand for
Family Allowances in the province of Quebec. So,
when this Family Allowance Act was under consideration in the House of Commons in 1944, I
stated that it was essentially a bribe offer to the
people of that province on the eve of the coming
provincial elections. ...I am not opposed to the
principle. Neither is the Progressive Conservative
Party. I would remind you that the Bill was eventually passed unanimously. ...I was and am
opposed to the way it was introduced, to the partisan motives which prompted it and to the way
the ill-digested measure was rushed to the House
in its dying hours without adequate consideration. ...during the past few days, a good many of

the Liberal candidates have given new evidence of the corrupt nature of the present Act by telling their electors how many thousands of dollars were coming to their ridings every month and every year when the Family Allowances begin to be paid. ...bread and circuses! ...under the Family Allowances Act Ontario pays out $43,500,000 a year more than she receives. Quebec will pay out $85,000,000... and will receive back about $84,000,000. ...in my judgment, we have gone at this whole problem in the wrong away. The soundest way of promoting family welfare throughout Canada is by using the Dominions' control over currency and over trade and commerce to provide first of all, the fullest employment possible, especially by providing the financial resources needed by low-cost housing in our urban and rural areas, and by subsidizing an adequate system of health services.[11]

He continued his crusade for affordable housing on July 3rd with a defence of those who needed it: "The assertion made by some irresponsible people that the slum dweller creates the slum is a libel on thousands of Canadian families whose only sin is that they must live in disgraceful surroundings because decent homes, within their means, have not been provided."[12]

Bruce was re-elected with a sound majority and the Conservatives increased the size of the Opposition.

* * * * *

Although Bruce would have snorted at the suggestion, he had become an excellent debater. He had even added some show-business-like presentations as he was able, with some appropriate posturing, to dramatize his ideas. He also had become adept at using reporters to expand his presentations, by humour, stringency, and wit, which drew reporters to his side. He enjoyed being a Member and was convinced that he was fighting the good fight.

NOTES

1. Bruce, H. A. *Varied Operations*. Longmans, Green, 1958 303.

2. *Canadian Hospital* 20:4:14.

3. Bruce Papers, Queen's University Archives.

4. *Globe and Mail*, July 31, 1944.

5. *The News*, August 1944.

6. *Globe and Mail*, August 2, 1944.

7. *Globe and Mail*, April 14, 1944.

8. *Ottawa Journal*, August 4, 1944.

9. Bruce Papers, Queen's University Archives.

10. Letter, Bruce to H. Farthing, December 8, 1945.

11. Radio Address, CFRB, Toronto.

12. Radio Address, CFCL, Toronto.

CHAPTER 12

Guns or Baby Bonuses

There were other veterans in the House, but Bruce seemed to be the one most focused on military matters. He had tackled the government on why Canada could not manufacture tanks and had won. His arguments to establish a "Canadian Air Force" had been successful. The House debates had brought out some of his finest constructive criticism. In the background there was always a leit-motif of insistence on the need for a system of health insurance. Although he had nothing but scorn for King's politicking, in and out of the House, he was generally calm and rational in his reasoning. His relentless pursuit of what he considered a poor war effort by Canada impelled his original reason for running for Parliament, because as he was refused enlistment to fight the Germans, he vowed that there would be Sturm und Drang in fighting the battles in the Commons at Ottawa.

At the end of WW1 the government took over and converted a factory on Christie Street to serve as a military hospital. It remained the major veteran's hospital until WW2, even though it abutted a railroad track, and was noisy, and dirty, and generally in poor repair. There was some relief from overcrowding by using the empty Chorley Park as a holding and convalescent unit.

Although there had not been large numbers of casualties up to the middle of 1943, Bruce and Drew realized that with the invasion of Europe the numbers would rise. In July of that year Bruce challenged Ian Mackenzie, Minister of Pensions and National Health, that the Christie Street Hospital was inadequate and that Canadian casualties deserved better. He stated that young men, sometimes 82 to a ward, had to lie in dust, filth, heat, and noise.

Mackenzie, still smarting from Bruce's previous Bren gun fusillade, replied that there was an adequate number of beds and added that there were plans to expand the building. Bruce became Parliamentary spokesperson for veterans' organizations, including The Canadian Corps Association, and for voluntary committees, mostly women, who were objecting to the Christie Street site and urged building a new veterans' hospital on Bayview Avenue.

While awaiting action on this matter Bruce revealed "discrepancies" in figures of army strength given by Defence Minister Ralston compared with those announced by the Wartime Information Board. Bruce contested the Minister's reports of army intake and disclosed that only 57 rather than 100 per cent had been inducted under the compulsory training law. This was patentedly short of what was needed.

"The idea of Canada being able to create and maintain an army overseas without conscription will prove to be a fantasy. It is difficult to understand how our government, which could not countenance conscription, would make commitments which it should have known it could not fulfill without conscription," he stated. He urged the removal "...of the hamstring clauses of the present Conscription Act." Ralston replied that the overseas pool of reinforcement was up to the estimated requirements and that behind the pool there were about 60,000 general service troops in Canada available for overseas, if required.[1]

Following D-day, the forecast that 50 per cent of

invasion troops would be casualties was realized, and Bruce again addressed Mackenzie, over the inadequacy of the Christie Street hospital. He deplored the fact that a motion made previously for the production of correspondence relating to Christie Street, had not been brought forward and "...was being deliberately held up." Mackenzie demanded that the word "deliberate" be withdrawn; however, the session closed before further action could be taken. By June, Bruce stated in a letter to the *The Globe and Mail* that "With ordinary foresight a new hospital building could have been erected and ready long ago." The building had been held up because an assistant to the Minister had inspected Christie Street hospital and felt that it was suitable. Bruce charged that the assistant had little idea of what was needed in a hospital and cited the problem of nervous patients in wards who could not get a full night's sleep because of the surrounding industrial noise. "In my judgment it is a manifestation of utter callousness to condemn the young wounded soldiers of this war to an environment and spectacle such as presently holds in the Christie Street hospital," he ended.[2]

In the same month, he told the House that a doctor could not use his stethoscope at Christie, because of the the noise of passing trains. In answer to Mackenzie's plan to enlarge the hospital, Bruce said, "...you will have committed an offence against the gallant boys, who are returning wounded and sick."

The next month he used a surgeon's scalpel to bare the facts that, although, as Mackenzie claimed, there were sufficient beds, there were not adequate facilities for operating. He had in his pocket a report from Drew, obtained by the Ontario government, of the number of Canadian soldiers in England who were awaiting prosthesis and could not possibly be fitted at Christie. These were clear overtones of his Report delivered in 1916 that amputees should be evacuated from England to Canada as soon as possible. Bruce brazenly advised the Prime Minister that he "...relieve the Minister of his office and get some competent, up-to-date earnest young man who will sincerely go about his job and provide what the soldiers require, that is, adequate, comfortable and modern equipment to look after them."

Mackenzie counter-attacked Bruce by citing McPhail's book and reminding the House that this was the man "...who was condemned for his own administration of hospital services."

Bruce replied by asking whether or not MacPhail had been relieved of his post as historian, "...because his first book was inaccurate and untrue." Mackenzie replied, "If he was so relieved he only shared the distinction of my honourable friend."[3]

The temperature of the House rose, Bren guns made their appearance, amid a catechism of other charges, until the Speaker demanded withdrawal of Mackenzie's remarks. This time there were no expulsions.

Part of the load at Christie Street was lightened by sending some casualties to the Toronto East General Hospital. Sunnybrook Hospital, built by the Department of Veterans' Affairs, did not open until after the war. Bruce received many congratulations on his stand, including one from Sidney Smith, President of the University of Manitoba, who observed that Mackenzie, "...in his private and public capacity, is no credit to his clan!".

While it was a clear victory for Bruce, he was not always so successful. One month earlier he had, according to *The Globe and Mail*[4], been "...the only member who had the courage to rise in defence of freedom of debate." This event followed on the dismissal of Senator T. D. Bouchard from the chairmanship of the Quebec Hydro Commission in retaliation for a speech he had made in the Senate. The Senator was dismissed by Quebec Premier A. Godbout after he attacked the Order of Jacques Cartier, and said there were some in French Canada who believed it was in their interest to create "not only a new French Province in Canada but an independent Catholic and French state." Such a statement was politically incorrect in the 1940's.

Bruce mounted a vigorous and uncompromising defence of the right of free speech and the right of Parliamentarians to speak freely without threat or fear of punishment. However the Speaker ruled that Bruce was out of order, on the basis that Standing Order no. 41 stated "no member shall refer to any debate in the Senate." Bruce objected to this with "I am just saying a word in defence of Freedom of Speech, and I am entitled to do so." An obviously angry Justice Minister St. Laurent stated, "Because the honourable member represents the constituency he does represent, he cannot flout the rules of Parliament and the ruling just given."

Bruce maintained in debating the Speaker, that Freedom of Speech had been denied to a member of Parliament and it was perfectly in order for Bruce to continue his remarks. The contretemps continued, with Bruce finally quoting Voltaire's statement, "I disagree with what you say, but I will defend to the death your right to say it." However, he had spent his force and had to bow to the Speaker.

While the surgeon was cutting a swath in the House, The Wellesley was reaping a poor harvest. In 1938 it reported a loss of $9,407, although, by a magnificent effort, it was able to reduce this by 90 per cent in 1939. However with the commencement of hostilities, nurses and doctors went off to war, and it was impossible to get staff. By January 1940 there was an overdraft of $35,000 and little prospect of meeting the bank call. A new Chairman of the Board, C. H. Carlisle, President of the Dominion Bank, warned that the institution would have to close; the only possible salvation was to give up its private status and become a public hospital. In preparation for this the outstanding bonds owned by Mulock and Edmund Osler were redeemed at 10 cents on the dollar. In truth, there had been no loss over the years as interest had been paid on the original investment. Bruce, who owned the majority of the stock, agreed to give up his without return. Estimates at that time placed his gift between $150,000, and several hundred thousands, counting the value of The Wellesley property. It was a generous move on his part as the federal government had already approached The Wellesley to see if it could be purchased for a military hospital. But Bruce, and the Board, agreed that the need for civilian beds was high and they preferred that The Wellesley be reserved for that use. In fact, there had been few casualties up to that date.

At the same time it was hoped that money could be raised privately to support the institution. This scenario never happened and by the middle of 1942 the Board advised that unless some help was received, the hospital would be closed by November 30th.

Political pressure was applied and the City of Toronto, which was one of the major users of any new public facility, voted a grant of $150,000 with a promise of $50,000 more, to be given when a planned new building, which provided new beds for public ward patients, was completed. This paradoxical situation that in the face of failure, The Wellesley was continuing to expand, set a pattern which lasted well into the latter part of the century. Despite imminent financial collapse, there was always an expansion program, designed to keep the hospital at the cutting-edge of medical care. Carlisle accepted the promise of $50,000 and launched a dream building plan of an ultra-modern, six-storey, 750-bed facility, with the hospital raising $350,000. At that time it was anticipated that a wealthy board member would make a major donation. However, as the six-storey building rose the prospects for the donation descended, and when the new wing opened in 1947 the Board faced an urgent need to raise $800,000.

This type of smoke-and-mirrors financing was not shared with The Wellesley staff. The nurses, considered to be one of the major assets of the hospital, did not realize how precarious was the future of the hospital. A new head of surgery, Dr. John Laing MacDonald, was appointed and, being an orthopedic surgeon, he began planning for bigger and better. Part of this scheme was to make The Wellesley a teaching hospital, and instead of being open to all physicians, privileges were to be reserved to University-appointed staff.

The fund-raising campaign fell short and the construction company threatened a suit to recover $193,000. To meet this new emergency a special committee of three, George McCullagh, Colonel W. A. Phillips, and J. G. Godsoe, was appointed as a rescue team.

The trio considered a number of propositions including selling The Wellesley Hospital to Mount Sinai. An alternative was considered when the Salvation Army showed an interest. However, the final resolution was spear-headed by McCullagh who approached the Government of Ontario with a win-

win plan. For a grant of $2 million to the Toronto General Hospital to pay The Wellesley debts, and at the same time to provide funds for an expansion of the General, The Wellesley would surrender its charter and become part of the General. The plan was not difficult to effect as Norman Urquhart, and one other member of The Wellesley Board, were on the Board of the General. This meant that The Wellesley would be a division of the General with some Board seats, but it was agreed that the Department of Nursing would remain responsible to The Wellesley manager. This was an agreeable solution to The Wellesley hospital staff because they were becoming full-fledged University appointees and the expansion plans would proceed. Part of the jubilation over preserving The Wellesley was diluted by the fact that the School of Nursing, and other staff members, had not been kept informed of the plans, and were disappointed that Herbert Bruce would no longer be head of the hospital.

In recognition of Bruce's services, when he was 80 years of age, a commemorative plaque, proposed by McCullagh, was placed in The Wellesley entrance hall. "Inasmuch as we are not burying The Wellesley Hospital but reviving it, it is natural that my thought should turn to what we owe Dr. Bruce," said McCullagh.

McCullagh was another meteoric figure who dazzled the political landscape from the late thirties to the fifties. He enrolled in that remarkable group of men who became special friends of Bruce. The doctor had an amazing ability to forge close relationships with men such as Mulock, Hughes, Beaverbrook, Manion, Meighen, Drew, and Diefenbaker. McCullagh fitted the pattern. Like many of the others, he was a self-made man, who sold papers in London, Ontario, when he was 9 years old and landed a salesman's job with *The Globe* in 1921. His ability was so persuasive that he earned bonuses every week and was able to peddle the paper in barren Liberal areas. One of his tactics was to challenge a farmer to a plowing contest. The prize went to the one who could plow the straighter furrow. The city slicker, who did not reveal that he was an excellent ploughman, usually won the prize — a newspaper subscription from the chagrined farmer. Bruce had a similar ability behind a horse and once beat a challenge from journalist Gordon Sinclair, by plowing a cleaner, straighter furrow.

McCullagh pyramided a job as a financial reporter into a Bay Street brokerage company and then found William H. Wright, who had discovered one of the richest gold mines in Canada. The consummate salesman who could sell a Tory newspaper to a hard-backed Grit had little trouble persuading multi-millionaire Wright to buy *The Globe* and then *The Mail and Empire* as a speculation. By this time McCullagh was able, with his own funds to add *The Telegram* to a newspaper empire, which now earned a fortune and became the major Conservative power in the country.

Bruce met McCullagh at a dinner in 1936 in the National Club, which was to celebrate the acquisition of the two papers, which had now become *The Globe and Mail*. "I shall never forget our first meeting... when the wise men from the east ventured to give advice to the young man of 32 as to how he should meet his new responsibilities," wrote the doctor in 1948. Bruce continued to describe that "...a new force had entered into the newspaper world. Next to Maxwell, I have an abiding interest in your health and future success, of which I have no doubt."

The concern for McCullagh's health was prescient

as a combination of a period of alcoholism, a driving psyche to succeed, and a lifestyle incompatible with well-being, meant that Bruce was, on many occasions, called upon to save the newspaperman's life.

Friendship flourished. George and his wife, Phyllis regularly socialized with Angela and Herbert, and were frequently joined by George and Fiorenza Drew for dinner parties or an evening at McCullagh's motion-picture room in his home at Thornhill. Occasionally young Maxwell joined the party. In truth, George McCullagh assumed a filial relationship with Bruce because his age was close to a natural sibling, while Maxwell was closer to the age of a grandson. It was reported that McCullagh invited Wright, when the idea of publishing a newspaper was first broached, to "Link arms and go on a crusade." The campaign began in 1939 when McCullagh, in a series of broadcasts launched the Leadership League, which was aimed at curbing wild government spending by abolishing provincial governments and setting up a national federal government. The combination of McCullagh's ability to convince and the package that he was selling, led to an enthusiastic response across the country. "Let George do it!" became a slogan which threatened all political parties as McCullagh was able to attract young people and convince them to take a greater interest in national affairs and to set up community discussion groups. The League called to the non-aligned to step forward and demand an end to the depression, improvement in social conditions, and a raising of the standard of living. This became a daily theme of the most powerful morning newspaper in Canada. Bruce was ecstatic, as the League was close on the heels of his messages while Lieutenant-Governor, and he accepted the post of Honorary Chairman. But the drain of energy with so extensive a program led to a breakdown in McCullagh's health. Bruce reported to Beaverbrook in 1940, "...too bad about G.McC dreadful luck... one reverse after another" The Leadership League gradually died, leaderless.

McCullagh and Beaverbrook had been brought together by Bruce, who had written to Cherkley describing the dynamic new figure on the Canadian newspaper scene. The two publishers had shared the platform, when they received honourary degrees at the U of T. In spite of having helped elect Hepburn in the late thirties, McCullagh was quite comfortable sitting with his conservative friends, because he had now become a front fighter for the Tories.

Naturally, Drew was present on this occasion. His friendship with Bruce went back to the thirties when the Conservative Party was attempting to un-seat Hepburn. Bruce had been foremost in supporting Drew, not only because of his political presence and his background, as he came from United Empire Loyalist stock in southwestern Ontario, but because he shared many principles with Bruce. He and his wife were frequent guests at Chorley Park and indeed were the last dinner guests before the end of Bruce's term. While Bruce was in the Federal House, he received frequent letters from Drew, when after Bruce was expelled from the House, Drew was quick to write a letter, "I only want to repeat what I told you this morning about my admiration for the course you followed yesterday, and to tell you that this opinion is shared by everyone to whom I have spoken today. I can recall very few instances where there was such a feeling of relief that someone had shown sufficient courage to stand up against the abominable steam roller tactics which have been employed in the House of Commons for several years."

Drew was of the same mind as Bruce on matters of conscription, and presented the figures which showed it would be impossible to continue to fight the war unless the draftees were available for active service overseas. At the same time he warned Bruce that the casualties in Normandy the previous week, had been horrific when the Black Watch of Montreal had been cut to pieces, including the death of the commander and 16 other officers.

He had also provided a great deal of background information for Bruce to continue his fight for a better accommodation for wounded soldiers, than was offered by Christie Street. He supplemented this advice with a letter to King, stating that "The building of a new military hospital accommodation is long over-due."

McCullagh and Bruce went to Washington in 1941 to hear Churchill address the combined Senate and Congress. At the same time they were able to meet with Beaverbrook, who accompanied the Prime Minister. Beaverbrook was impressed by McCullagh and this feeling was reinforced by many letters from Bruce to Beaverbrook in which he extolled McCullagh's abilities.

"It was only under pressure that I accepted the last nomination and that I was free to resign whenever I felt disposed to do so," stated Bruce on May 17, 1946, when he was explaining to his deskmate George Black, MP, why he was leaving the party. The pressures on him at his age were simply too much, especially the commute by train to Ottawa because he was unable to sleep on the coaches. In addition, Maxwell was coming home and Bruce wanted to resume normal family relations. He had sold the farm and the entire Ayrshire herd the previous year because of difficulty in getting proper help.

But there was still much to do before he left the House. He continued his work with the Canadian Corps Association and was a spokesperson in the House from the opposition side, for improved terms of rehabilitation for soldiers and casualties. In January of 1944 he had urged the establishment of the Department of Veterans Affairs which was in line with the way the Ministry felt.

Bruce's interest had a personal aspect, as he was anxious to have Maxwell repatriated as early as possible. The original Army plan was to have been "first in, first out," but when this scheme collapsed, Bruce contacted Beaverbrook to see if something could be done for Maxwell. In a heartfelt letter he pointed out that Maxwell had served in the United Kingdom, Italy, and the Netherlands and had been mentioned in dispatches, ending his active service with the rank of major. He had the unique opportunity to fire the two 15-inch guns of the Royal Naval *Monitor Roberts* in the Sicily landings, this gun platform had last been engaged in warfare at Gallipoli in 1915. Soon, Maxwell was returned to Canada and enrolled in Osgoode Hall Law School; because like many sons of eminent doctors, he chose not to follow in his father's giant footsteps.

When Dr. Brock Chisholm was appointed Deputy Minister of Health in 1944, Bruce was heartened. For the first time a physician, albeit Chisholm was a psychiatrist, had been put in charge of health problems in Canada. Chisholm had an excellent record for organization, when he had been head of the Army's Medical Services during the latter part of WW2. He stressed, and Bruce was in agreement, that it was no longer feasible to consider a specific person with a specific disease, but that the patient must be taken in context of his total environment. Chisholm had espoused this approach and had been adamant to develop social medicine, which he opined benefited many. Bruce in his work on the Special Committee on Social Security was in accord with the principle. However, Chisholm was well ahead of his time and sometimes set the bottoms and the teeth of his audience on edge. Primarily he stressed that many people who imagined themselves to be suffering from physical ailments, had only mental disturbances. Part of this was caused by the insistence of parents raising children as little gentlemen and ladies with repression of the basic human instincts. Chisholm prophesied that this type of upbringing would only lead to more wars, and that it was necessary to teach the children to think for themselves, rather than having the parents make all the decisions.

Having been wounded when an infantry-man in WW1, he had developed a horror of war and its unprecedented casualties. His regiment, the 48th Highlanders, had sustained many severely wounded and this was stamped indelibly on the young Captain Chisholm's mind.

One of his main aims was to prevent future war and he saw that the only way to do so was to show children how to explore their minds, and find the truth. If parents continued to teach children fairytales, and did not teach them how to think, the result was inevitable.

His passion to teach the "truth" rather than legend led to a great public reaction when he warned that it might be necessary to sacrifice Santa Claus, "a national myth", for the sake of the future of the country. His reasoning was that if children were taught something which was shown to be false, that they lost faith in the future. He looked at this philosophy as being within the realm of psychiatry, whose mission was to prevent war in the future.

Having announced that children should not be taught a ridiculous story such as how Santa Claus could come down the chimney carrying a refrigerator, Chisholm evoked a massive storm of protest over all the country. While a few agreed with the general principle that children should not be taught falsehoods, the majority felt that the myth was non-harmful.

Chisholm, a spell-binding orator, was able to expand on the need for logic and reason as opposed to myths and falsehoods and produced a coruscating cascade of calumny:

> Misguided by authoritarian dogma, bound by exclusive faith, stunted by inculcated loyalty, torn by frantic heresy, bedeviled by insistent schism, drugged by ecstatic experience, confused by conflicting certainty, bewildered by invented mysteries, and loaded down by the weight of guilt and fear engendered by its own original premises, the unfortunate human race, deprived by these incubi of its only defenses and its only reasons for striving, its reasoning power and its natural capacity to enjoy the satisfaction of its natural urges, struggles along under its ghastly self-imposed burden.[5]

This was more than enough to stir the old warrior, Bruce, into rising in the House and thundered that Chisholm's creed "shocked the Christian conscience of the country."[6] He explained that he felt duty bound, as a medical man, to disagree with the American Psychiatric Association, which supported the Deputy Minister. Bruce rarely lost his cool during his speeches but on this occasion he glowed, and moulded Chisholms' attack on myths into a campaign against the clergy. Chisholm, although religious, was a strong critic of the church, which he felt should be more practical. One of his favoured targets in organized religion was its opposition to issuing condoms to the troops during WW2.

Chisholm became the man who did not believe in Santa Claus. In spite of uproars in the House, and across the country, he did not resign, particularly as Mackenzie King pronounced he was happy with his service. Bruce shook his head in despair.

Like Sam Hughes, forty years previously, Chisholm was making speeches that caused a great deal of embarrassment to the government. Fortunately, an opportunity arose to rid the country of this troublesome anti-priest. The newly formed international Interim Health Committee, which oversaw the World Health Organization, needed an executive secretary. Louis St. Laurent was happy to announce that Chisholm had accepted the appointment, and had resigned as Deputy Minister of Health.

Once again Bruce received many congratulations on his stand from individuals and organizations across Canada. The Societé St-Jean Baptiste du Québec hastened to congratulate him for "Defending Christian principles against Chisholm."

It was almost his last major effort in the House. But he reserved one last moment for demonstrating, once again, that he was his own man — and could still surprise and confound.

On March 30, 1946, he wrote to John Bracken to say that he had tendered his resignation to the Speaker. He explained to Bracken that he had yielded to an urgent request to stand but with the end of the war and the completion of demobilization, two of the main reasons for which he had entered the House no longer remained. He preferred that a veteran, whose experience during the war would give him special qualifications for further service to his country, could take his place.

Bruce timed his resignation so that it reached the Speaker during the evening break, thus scooping the daily papers and permitting *The Globe and Mail* to have a clear announcement. He made sure that the reporter received a copy at the same time as the Speaker, who read the announcement to the House that evening, in accordance with parliamentary custom. The news came to Parliament as a complete surprise, and Bracken, after the Speaker sat down, read a personal letter received from Bruce explaining his motives.

There was a Canada-wide tribute to Bruce. *The Globe and Mail* reported: "In less time than it takes many members to make their maiden speech, Dr. Bruce was nationally known for a quality all too rare in our public men, his great moral courage. ...It was his voice which rose clearly above the howls of the government benches to protest the wrongful internment of innocent aliens... never once did he compromise his principles, never did he abandon that for which he fought."[7] Another report pointed out that "...should be considered only as another step in a remarkable career. For years perhaps the most eminent surgeon in Toronto with — what is rare enough in that profession — a genius for organization, he made an international reputation as a war surgeon in the First World War. ...The House loses a peppery, picturesque and able member."

The Ottawa Journal editorialized: "To his mind, conviction was more important than applause for comforting platitudes, conscience more worth while than desk-thumping of colleagues. ...Our House of Commons in recent years has been too stuffy with 'dignity'. In trying to get away from billingsgate, product of dunces, it has swung over to too much pillow fighting, product of dullness and dishonesty".[8]

But there was not a universal admiration for this member who "Didn't court popularity". The Prime Minister charged that Bruce's resignation was a "course which may establish a dangerous precedent. The *House of Commons Act*, prescribing a way in which a member may resign, cannot have intended to make resignation easy and applicable on the slightest provocation," King contended. "Unless there are grave reasons compelling him to return to private life or he received some appointment from the Crown, he is, I believe in bounded duty to keep the mandate he has received from his constituents."[9]

Bracken lost no time in countering that Dr. L. MacDiarmid, member elect from Glengarry after the 1945 election, had yielded his seat after King's defeat in Prince Albert. *The Telegram* took King's remarks to be an indirect criticism of Bruce and set many parliamentary minds searching for precedents which could be found for the resignation of Dr. Bruce. There was no shortage and Bruce received a great number of congratulatory letters which decried the Prime Minister's pettiness. Bruce ended the affair with a letter:

> King seems to be upset by my resignation. What a hypocritical statement he made when he said: 'It was dangerous precedent,' in view of the fact that he himself had got into the House on some three occasions by having a member resign his seat. Of course, it is quite alright to have them do this for Mackenzie King, but it would be very improper to do it for a soldier who had served in the last war. Having failed to serve in any way, he

does not understand what it means to have the soldier's viewpoint represented in the House.

Beaverbrook, who received the letter, was appreciative.

One of Bruce's most treasured letters was received from Gladys Dudley, his secretary in the House:

> I have been trying to make myself believe of late that I am "shock proof", but your letter this morning leaves me entirely unconvinced. What an "April Fool joke" you played on me. And, what wouldn't I give to look upon it as such!
>
> ...You have richly earned the leisure which retirement will bring to you and should not be deprived of the comforts of your home and the companionship with your family. Nevertheless I cannot bring myself to say that I wish it for you this session.
>
> You certainly have made history for the short length of time you have been here but I would have preferred you as a permanent tenant — in view of the housing shortage.

* * * * *

In entering Parliament Bruce found the platform for which he had searched unwittingly for many years. As Lieutenant-Governor he could reach many people, but as an MP, all Canadians could hear his thoughts. His opposition to the manner in which family allowances were hurried through the House, presaged thoughts of later observers on the speed and compulsiveness of vote-seeking politicians as they propelled the country into a welfare state. His enthusiasm for public housing became embodied in various agencies. A comprehensive national medical insurance plan, which he planned and proposed, finally became a reality, although the wisdom of his urging that there should be personal contributions was not appreciated for some years.

CHAPTER 12

1. *Globe and Mail*, February 29, 1944.

2. Ibid., July 20, 1944.

3. Ibid., August 13, 1944.

4. Ibid., July 3, 1944.

5. Ottawa Journal, November. 6, 1945.

6. The *Toronto Telegram*, December. 12, 1945.

7. Globe and Mail, April 2, 1946.

8. Ottawa Journal, April 3, 1946.

9. The *Toronto Telegram*, April 7, 1946.

The letters quoted in this chapter are in the Bruce Papers, Queen's University Archives.

CHAPTER 13

Peace Returns — for Some

Having retired from public life, Bruce could now concentrate on personal matters. When he was in Ottawa, he realized that he no longer required his old residence/office on Bloor Street and determined to sell. One of the first people he approached was Ontario Premier Tom Kennedy whose government planned to erect a Workmen's Compensation Board building in the area. There was some competition with this particular site as some MPPs favoured a lakefront location, close to Union Station, because many workers came from the north, and building close to the railway would be more convenient. Bruce, in his bid to sell the building, drew up a comparison of the two locations in which the lakefront site ran a poor second to his Bloor Street property. In preparing this comparison, Bruce went to a great deal of trouble to get advice on pilings for the buildings. They were much more extensive in the lakefront property, and the facilities which would be offered at the lakefront would not be able to have underground rooms. He presented this statement of facts to the Ontario Government and awaited an answer. However, when no response had arrived by August 1949, Bruce addressed the new Premier, Leslie Frost, adding that he would undertake the demolition of the building property at no expense to the Ontario Government. Frost said consideration would be given and he deeply appreciated the factual material which Bruce had provided.

To strengthen the attractiveness of the proposition Bruce pointed out that Kennedy had made a definite commitment to purchase the Bloor Street property. He forwarded to Frost particulars of the property and quoted a price of $15.00 per foot. Apparently Kennedy had said this price was "right." By November the 29th of that year the Provincial Police expressed an interest in purchasing the property and made a visit. At that time Frost asked how soon the tenants could be moved out and Bruce replied they were on a month's notice and that the building could be empty as soon as needed.[1]

As the business dragged on, Bruce became exasperated and on January 7, 1950, rang Frost at his home in Lindsay to ask if he intended to purchase the property. Frost's answer was, "Yes, subject to the price being satisfactory."

Maybe Bruce was becoming a little irascible in his advanced years or possibly he was becoming fed up with political doublespeak. On January 31st he wrote to the Frost, saying:

> During a long lifetime I've had satisfactory and pleasant relations with many important (and busy) men, including Mr. Hepburn, and it seems incomprehensible that I should have to come to my own province and the leader of my own party to experience totally unbusiness-like methods as well as the discourteous treatment I received from you during the last seven months.
>
> I do not wish to discuss the Bloor St. property further with you or the incompetent advisors upon whom you rely.[2]

This drew an answer from Frost who acknowledged the long delay with, "There appears to have been

slowness on my part in coming to a decision." Frost
agreed that it was an impressive site and that several
of his departments had considered it. "One of the
greatest attractions to your property was the practically immediate possession, and I was trying to work
things out on a temporary basis which would avoid
committing ourselves to a building project which
would not fit into overall requirements."[3]

The milk of human kindness, which Bruce had
advocated in his earlier years, had somehow turned
to vinegar in his veins. He snarled back at Frost:

> Your letter of February 1st is in no sense an
> answer to mine of January 31st, nor am I
> impressed by your newly discovered reasons for
> taking months to decide about the Bloor St.
> property.
>
> Thoroughly tired out and disgusted by your
> tardiness in reaching a decision, I sold the prop-
> erty on January 30th, over the telephone, in ten
> minutes, for the price asked you, $15.00 per foot.
>
> I've only recapitulated a small part of the seem-
> ingly endless delays of being pushed around and
> the humiliations suffered at your hands, the like
> of which I have never experienced here before
> and which I greatly resent.[4]

A copy of this was sent to retired Tom Kennedy.

It was quite a feisty performance on Bruce's part.
Although he still retained many connections with
power in high places, there was always an advantage
to have the premier of the province on your side.

While Bruce was demonstrating how thorny he
could be, he was also negotiating in a benelovent
mode with a number of his colleagues to open the
Caven Memorial Research Foundation. Caven had
been a lifelong friend in The Wellesley Hospital, when
he and Bruce were acting as a team in the twenties

and thirties. After his death his widow maintained friendship with the Bruces and on her death, 10 years after husband's, she left $100,000 as a memorial. The money was designed to operate a research unit with Dr. R. J. Macmillan, Hugh McLaughlin, Q.C., and Bruce designated as trustees. It was stipulated that only the interest from the money should be used and that there should be no significant draw on the capital. Bruce was able to increase the funding by a commitment from J. S. McLean of Canada Packers for $15,000 per year for 5 years for operating expenses. In addition Percy Gardiner agreed to donate money for operations.

It was necessary for some expert legal work because Mrs. Caven had left the money to The Wellesley Hospital, but The Wellesley Hospital was now part of the General. This problem was solved by an agreement with Norman Urquhart, Chairman of the Board of the General.

The opening ceremonies were held on November 23, 1949, at the site of the Research Foundation and, naturally, Bruce had arranged for a visiting dignitary to cut the ribbon — the Right Honourable Lord Webb-Johnson, President of the Royal College of Surgeons of England, who was staying with Bruce at the time.

Dr. Gordon Murray was appointed Director of Research. He was a well-known surgeon and researcher in Canada, having successfully pioneered the "blue baby" operation at The Wellesley and also developed the prototype of an artificial kidney.

Bruce's association with Murray went back several years. When Gallie was about to retire from the position of Professor of Surgery, Bruce had put Murray's name forward as a candidate. However Gallie had decided that Robert Janes was the best choice. His appointment was passed, in spite of the urging by

Eric Phillips that Murray was a better choice. It was said, outside the committee room, that Gallie had said, "he would be damned if he would let some glass-blower choose his successor." Phillips was President of Research Enterprises Ltd., which had an enormous contract with the government to provide optical glass and range finders during the war.

Bruce had his usual fall-back position and proposed that Murray should be appointed as Professor of Experimental Research Surgery. In order to bolster this proposition he had arranged for a $15,000 donation from J. S. Maclean of Canada Packers to support the position. However, the recently appointed Dean of Medicine, J. Macfarlane, insisted that all surgery should be under one person, namely, Janes, with the result that the Bruce initiative was refused. Murray, meanwhile, had informed the committee that he would not accept the position unless it was established as a separate department. While Bruce was able to emphasize the desire to make provision for recognition of some of the younger surgeons of outstanding ability, the selection Board accepted his statements and agreed it would welcome suggestions which would provide greater scope for talents of men such as Murray.

At the opening ceremonies Webb-Johnson emphasized that some of the greatest discoveries in medicine had been made by men with very meagre resources and lacking great concentration of research establishments. Bruce echoed this approach by stating that research, "...will be carried on with complete freedom, the investigator being responsible only to the Caven trustees." There was a hidden agenda in these statements as it was well known that Murray had been refused access to the University's Banting laboratories and had had to use his own private funds to perfect his artificial kidney at a cost of more than $8000. By using the terms of the Caven will, it was possible to set up the research facility, independent of the University and the General.

Murray was working on a thesis that he could develop a horse serum to prevent or control female breast cancer. His team of researchers included a Dr. Holden, two technicians, and a cleaning staff. It was necessary to hire a stable for the horse. Although Murray was a busy surgeon, the research seemed to go well but he was frequently absent for international meetings. For example, in 1953 he attended meetings in Lisbon and was absent for almost two months.

By 1955 he presented a paper at the Toronto Academy of Medicine which outlined his success in treating twelve women with cancer of the breast. In his presentation he stated that the idea of "...developing the horse serum originated in my mind when I was doing pathology in England and that with modest help from the Caven Memorial Research Foundation, I was able to do his work." This was seen as a rather unhappy statement as the major thrust of the Foundation had been to support Murray.

By that time the five-year commitment from Maclean was terminated with his death. A handwritten memo for the Foundation Board specified there was some disappointment in the results and the Board decided to discontinue the facility, because of lack of supporting funds. It was felt that Murray could make arrangements with Percy Gardiner to finance ongoing work through a new institute.

Bruce decided that the Caven Fund should continue to be made available for financing medical research by turning it over to the U of T, where there was a movement to establish a Department of Biophysics, which would be centred in the Ontario

Cancer Institute. Macfarlane was anxious to recruit a head of the department and selected Dr. Arthur Ham. The money was turned over with the provision that the income would be used to provide Caven Fellowships at either graduate or post-doctorate level. Ham, in accepting the donation, wrote, "I am sure that the income will be exceedingly well-spent and be productive of much finer research."[5]

Bruce's disappointment at the failure of his research project was great. However it did not match his sorrow of the year of 1952.

On August 13th he wrote to Anthony Eden, whom he had met previously in London before Churchill stepped down, to advise him of the death of George McCullagh.

> It is with a heavy heart I give you some details of the death of my dear friend George. As you know he has been struggling with a painful and relentless nervous illness for about ten years, with periodic remissions during which time he carried on with great energy and ability, his newspapers, as well as sparing time to give initiative and drive to hospital campaigns and the work of the Governors of the Universities. He had just returned home, apparently much improved after three months treatment in an American hospital, when he succumbed the following day to a heart attack.

It was with bent shoulders that the normally erect Bruce attended the funeral services in St. Paul's. He carried a treasured letter that he had written in 1950 which read, "I should add that some time ago, he [McCullagh] told a mutual friend, that regardless of what happened, he can never cease loving me!!! So I accepted his proffered hand of friendship." There had been an unusual, fine relationship between these two men.

But it was unlikely that Bruce would not recover his enthusiasm and zest for life and resume activities. Although he had agreed that The Wellesley Hospital should unite with the General, the arrangement had been made at gun-point. Now there had been some recovery of confidence by The Wellesley staff and Bruce wrote to Frost in 1957, "...about the anomalous situation that had developed when The Wellesley Hospital became The Wellesley Division of the Toronto General Hospital and the latter took over its administration." He explained that the two institutions were far apart and the administration consisted of a weekly visit by the Director of the General. The end of the letter suggested there should be a separation of the two hospitals.[6]

It was remarkable, after the scorching letter he had sent to Frost just a short time previously, that now he was asking for special consideration for The Wellesley.

Frost replied (in five days!) that "The operation of The Wellesley division has for a number of years presented problems. One of the difficulties, of course, of setting up a separate institution is the administration, in which we had to start from scratch. That can be an expensive business. I will give this consideration within the next short time."[7]

Meanwhile, two members of The Wellesley, Doctors I. B. Macdonald and Neil Watters of the surgical staff, had approached an influential businessman in Galt to make a presentation to the Premier. This was made one year after Bruce's letter. Watters, in particular, was concerned about the fact that there was an "absentee landlord administration."

In 1959 Frost accepted an invitation to address the

nurses' graduation and, in his usual quiet way, announced that The Wellesley would now be a separate institution. This amputation of one of the General's appendages caused a great deal of anger on the General's Board, which had not been warned of the plan.

The Wellesley staff was delighted. I. B. Macdonald wired to Watters, who was vacationing in Venice that "The Frost has melted and our new plant will soon be blooming." Watters had no difficulty with the code and wired in return, "So glad the garden is doing well."

And well it did. Harold Turner took over as the Chairman of the new Wellesley Board in January 1960 and immediately announced that the original building of The Wellesley, which still served as a patient area, would be demolished and replaced by a modern structure, complete with outpatient facilities and laboratories.

Bruce lost no time in thanking Frost for his consideration, who replied, "I might say that what you said a year ago influenced my judgment in this matter."

This healing of the Bloor Street wound was completed when in 1960 Bruce congratulated Frost on calling for an inquiry into the cost of medications. Bruce had serious concern that overpricing of simple medications was causing considerable distress to the poor. This letter was followed by another in 1961 when the aging surgeon applauded the action of Frost in reducing the budget of Dr. Gordon Bates.

Bruce and Bates had a running feud dating from WW1. Bates was another health crusader who carved a place in Ontario circles by forming a Public Health League on the basis of fighting the "...scourge of venereal disease." While Bruce was advocating newer treatment programs for affected soldiers in England,

Bates set up an army unit in Canada along similar lines. He proselytized in the press against prostitutes and enrolled journalists to publicize how VD was destroying the lives of countless men, women, and children. It was not an easy task because many prominent citizens branded him as "sex mad" and "filthy minded." J. Atkinson, the publisher of *The Toronto Star*, refused to go to any meetings when Bates was speaking. But the rough-and-tumble zealot persisted and convinced Ottawa to grant funds to the provinces to set up diagnostic and treatment centres. His funding for the League came from prominent citizens and, to supplement the income, Bates persuaded a Hollywood producer to make a film about the disease, "Damaged Lives", which Bates directed. It became a great success but as it treated a delicate subject, mixed audiences were not permitted. The advertisement read for male or female audiences only. Children under 18 not permitted. His flamboyant lifestyle, including driving a custom-built Packard touring car which had been constructed for the Prince of Wales, incited much adverse comment, but he became known in many countries throughout the world and gradually assembled an organization devoted to prevention. His publicity claimed that he had initiated control of diphtheria in Toronto so that it was the first major city to have a complete year without a single case. He also asserted that he personally had persuaded Hepburn to enact the pasteurization of milk Bill. Of course, the province was replete with various people who claimed taking Hepburn by the arm and showing him tubercular children — and were the main force in getting pasteurized milk into the province's dairies.

Bates brazenly invaded the territory that Bruce had staked out by presenting a plan for better housing for the poor. He also tried to be appointed to the King George V Cancer Fund Board, which Bruce chaired. The Lieutenant-Governor was adamant that he wanted no interference from the self-appointed inter-loper and in 1936 wrote a letter to Bates:

...there is much duplication in social services and I can see no need for the so-called Health Leagues of Canada... We have a great many organizations, both medical and social which are doing splendid work and I feel the health of the people is being thoroughly well looked after... This is a small country and we have not a super abundance of wealthy people to call upon and in my opinion those we have, have been generous in their support of the existing organizations, who must necessarily suffer from appeals made from yet another organization.[9]

One of the super-abundant people, Sir James Woods, a League member, quickly defended Bates, provoking a prickly response from Bruce, who dis-sected a number of shaky pretensions to innovation which were part of the League's claims and stated that "The health of our citizens is being thoroughly safe-guarded."

But Sir James was not to be put off and sent a detailed rebuttal of Bruce's original letter. This time the reply was from G. P. Dymond, Bruce's secretary, and read: "...His Honour is astounded at the base-less charge... ." In addition Bruce, "...is astounded at your presumption." The debate gradually ran down, terminating with Woods resignation from the League in 1940. Bates continued his efforts, which now had world-wide impact, chiefly through a maga-zine, Health, to the end of the sixties. Bruce main-tained his mind-set and in 1961 informed Frost that Bates was a "parasite".[10]

* * * * *

The old lion still had sound teeth and strong opinions as demonstrated in his actions with Frost. But he was slowing down and most of his protestations were on smaller issues. His horizon was gradually shrinking.

Notes

From the Queen's University Archives:
1. Letter, Bruce to Frost, August 15, 1949.
2. Letter, Bruce to Frost, Jan. 21, 1950.
3. Letter, Frost to Bruce, Feb. 1, 1950.
4. Letter, Bruce to Frost, Feb. 6, 1950.
5. Letter, Ham to R. J. MacMillan, March 17, 1958.
6. Letter, Bruce to Frost, May 22, 1957.
7. Letter, Frost to Bruce, May 28, 1957.
8. Letter, Frost to Bruce, May 25, 1959.

From the P. Wysong Collection:
9. Letter, Bruce to Bates.
10. Letter, Bruce to Frost.

CHAPTER 14

The Last Battlefield

In addition to his many other activities and roles, Bruce clearly enjoyed his University connection. He was appointed to the U of T Board of Governors in 1931 and remained a member until his death, although he tried to resign on three occasions. During WW2 he served on the Connaught Laboratory Committee and enthused over the ability to produce anti-toxins and other biologicals for the war effort. The Banting bequest of insulin to the people of the world, foregoing any royalties or patents, meant the Connaught was always answering appeals, and modifying the product depending on current knowledge. In 1944, because of unexpected expenses associated with the purchase of the old Knox College property to allow expansion of Connaught's productivity, Bruce ensured that a special expenditure of $300,000 was approved by the University.

About the same time Premier Drew was concerned that the University would not be able to handle the expected influx of veterans at the end of the war, and suggested a re-organization of the governance of the institution. Bruce recommended a committee headed by U of T, Board of Governors Balmer Neilly, the President of McIntyre Porcupine Mines, to smooth relations between the government and the University.

Bruce shared his concerns with Drew about an impending major problem in the University. Mulock had been Chancellor since 1924. His was an hon-

orary position and although he had no authority over
the President, who was in effect the Chief Executive
Officer, Mulock presided over the Board of Governors.
On paper the Chancellor was elected by the graduates or the Alumni Federation, but in practice no one
ever stood against an incumbent. The Board sat as
trustees for the government and carried the full
weight of the province which granted the major funding. Buried in the constitution of the University was a
Statute which stated that if the Chancellor died while
in office he was to be replaced by the President, until
the end of a four-year term.

Cody was the President and at the age of 75 was 10
years over retirement age, which had removed his
two predecessors from office. In Bruce's words he
was "failing", but he refused to retire because at the
time of his appointment, no age limit was mentioned.

Bruce, McCullagh, and Drew saw that Simcoe Hall,
the nerve centre of the University, was slowly drifting
into a mausoleum mode as the chief policy-makers
approached a combined age of almost two centuries.
To lubricate the slide into a slough, the Principal of
University College, whose term was due to expire in
June 1944, contributed to the general deterioration
by slowly fading away.

Cody, made aware of the oncoming problem, after a
committee meeting with Bruce and other Senate and
Board members, approached Sidney Smith, President
of the University of Manitoba, requesting him to take
the Principalship of University College on a temporary basis, until a more suitable candidate could be
chosen from returning veterans. In the interim,
Smith was also to act as assistant to the President so
that he might learn the job, and move into it when
Cody, who never admitted to any constraint of his
tenure, decided to resign. That event was forecast for

a year in the future. While it was quite within the authority of the President to name the Principal, it was beyond his jurisdiction to appoint a President. This was the job of the Senate, on recommendation of the Board of Governors.

At the beginning of 1944, in anticipation of the imminent changes, Bruce wrote to Massey, High Commissioner for Canada in London, suggesting that, after a discussion with McCullagh and Neilly, that both agreed that they will have to face very soon a successor to the President. "When I proposed you as in every way qualified for the post, it was met with a hearty response... it has been quite clear to most of us that Dr. Cody could not continue for very long as he has been slipping badly and there was general feeling in the Board that the matter was considered urgent and perhaps will be admitted by the present incumbent."[1]

Massey, who was scheduled to end his term that year, replied that he was honoured and touched.[2] However, by that time Cody had played his card and Smith was directly in line for the presidency. Bruce, who usually had a fall-back position, then suggested that Massey should be named Chancellor. Once again he was able to support his suggestion with enthusiastic agreement from Drew, McCullagh, and Neilly. Remarkably, Bruce was able to conduct the negotiations in this arena, although he was in the process of being expelled from the House in Ottawa.

In agreeing that he would permit his name to stand, Massey stipulated that he would not run against Mulock.[3] But the pertinent questions at that time were whether Mulock was fit to serve another term, and whether he had the desire. Eric Phillips, recently appointed to the U of T Senate, reported that he had spoken with Arthur Fleming, President of the

Alumni Federation, who recounted that Mulock had indicated to Cody that he would like to "die in office," and that the one thing he had his heart set on, was to be re-elected in September. The Federation then completed papers for his nomination. Mulock had grown old in the service of his country, and at 104 years, though a noble figure, he was almost senile. His rare appearances at Board meetings confirmed to Bruce and McCullagh that he was incapable of continuing. Bruce, in a letter to Drew on July 22nd, recalled the *University Act* which stated that if the incumbent died, the President would automatically become the Chancellor. "I am sorry to have to express the opinion that I believe this suggestion has risen into the mind of the President himself who would like, above all things, to continue his association with the University by becoming Chancellor."[4]

Cody, who had asked the Alumni Federation to nominate Mulock, was playing on their hopes that they would finally realize their long agitation for an election of a Chancellor by the graduates, would bear fruit. Apparently they were not aware of the fact that the Senate had passed the Statute which had the very opposite effect, if Mulock died in office.

Bruce, who had been told by Mulock that he had no further interest in the University[5] (contrary to another person's recollections), proceeded to draw up the nomination papers for Massey, and, "Knowing of the admiration that Sir William has always had for Vincent, I thought it would be very nice to have him sign his nominating paper, and with this subject in view, called on him." Apparently Mulock was favourable to this suggestion but said he couldn't sign the paper, until he had a talk with Cody. Because the latter was out of town at his cottage, Bruce sent the nomination to Cody, asking for his signature.

Cody replied, "I do not think I should sign anyone's nomination papers at present. Indeed, I am doubtful as to the wisdom of the President taking any public part in the Chancellor's election."[6] At the same time he directed A. B. Fennell, registrar for the University, to cable to Massey, pointing out that he and Mulock had been nominated for the office of Chancellor. Fennell then reminded Massey of the Statute which said that "No person shall be eligible for election as Chancellor unless he is a resident of Ontario and that the right of any person to be Chancellor, if questioned, shall be finally decided by the Senate." This cable provoked two responses from Bruce. The first was that he almost withdrew Massey's nomination, as Massey was unwilling to enter an election in opposition to Mulock. The second response was to question by whose authority the letter had been sent to Massey? Neilly, at the Board of Governors meeting on September 14th, indicated that Fennell's cable, "I regret to say, gives rise to a situation that merits the serious consideration of this Board... the cable above referred to was, or any rate could be, considered as an affront to a graduate of this University."[7] While acknowledging that the Senate was quite entitled to examine and pass upon the qualifications for the office of Chancellor, he questioned whether the same examination should not apply to all candidates, including Mulock.

It was also put forward at that meeting that Massey was overseas on government business but had a permanent residence at Port Hope, Ontario, with a staff of servants, and should be considered a resident of the province.

Neilly had assembled his facts and arguments largely through the work of Bruce who had demanded from the registrar a copy of the cable that had been sent to Massey. Bruce recounted the whole matter to Drew when he also revealed that several members of the Alumni Federation had visited Mulock, who was confused and obviously close to the end of his life. On September 12 he wrote to Massey with a report of a meeting he had had with Neilly, Cody, and the Chairman of the Board, Dr. Bruce Macdonald. They had discussed the impasse and Bruce had suggested that Cody could very easily relieve the situation by calling on Sir William and suggesting to him that he withdraw. "This seemed to annoy him very much and he replied that he was not going to be made the goat."[8] This inability to move either Cody or the Chairman of the Board, was the trigger to Bruce withdrawing Massey's name at almost the last moment. Mulock was elected Chancellor — and died nineteen days later. Cody resigned as president and was appointed Chancellor by the Senate. Smith became president of the University.

This domino game should have ended the matter; however, Bruce still had some tiles on the table. He and Neilly pursued Macdonald, who had been directed by the Board to apologize to Massey over the offending cable. Bruce secured a copy of the letter which Macdonald sent which simply tried to exonerate Fennell and did not offer an apology. At the next meeting Macdonald was censured by the Board and in a short time reported that, on medical advice, he was forced to resign as Chairman.

Next, the Senate repealed the Statute that had paved the way for Cody to be elevated to Chancellor.

Bruce memorialized the labyrinthine activities which had lead to the results on December 28, 1944, to be spread in the minutes.[9] On January 12, 1945, more tortuosity was added to the history when Bruce learned that Cody had advised Massey that he would not be successful in his candidacy as Sir William was determined to "die in harness." Bruce added that if Massey had been aware of the imminent demise of the Chancellor, he would have let his name stand.[10]

By May 1946 the new Board Chairman, Eric Phillips, formed a committee to consider revision of the *University Act*. Amidst the business considered was a presentation by Bruce regarding the Chancellorship in which he outlined procedures carried out at other institutions. His comments were given hand-in-hand with those of the Alumni Federation and led to some revisions. It was decided that no one who was in receipt of funds from the University could stand as Chancellor. Cody was receiving a pension for his years of service. Further deliberations led to a shortening of the term of office from four to three years. Cody objected to this provision and claimed in a statement in *The Star* on April 29, 1947, "that the new Statute had been rushed through without proper discussion". Nevertheless Phillips pressed on and at the end of three years of Cody's office, asked a committee of representatives of the Senate, the Board, and the Alumni to recommend a new Chancellor. Cody was defeated and Massey took office.

Although the Board minutes were not open, Cody, through a series of newspaper interviews, brought his case to the public. *The Financial Post* wrote,

> The fight over the Chancellorship of the University of Toronto is going to leave deep scars. Almost everybody will welcome to that place of honour the Right Honourable Vincent Massey. But only a few will excuse his shabby scheming which put Dr. Cody out of the post a year before

expiry of the term for which he was appointed. The Chancellorship is truly honorary. There was no reason whatever for rushing a new appointment. Dr. Cody had been closely linked with the University for almost two generations. During a long career of public service he stood for all things the University is to stand for. The strong-arm tactics of the Board of Governors in casting him out are just crude. It appears that three members of the Board of Governors have violent personal antagonism for Cody. Others on the board found themselves swept along in this inept, graceless bungle... The Cody incident suggests that the Board of Governors are all appointees of the provincial government ambitious to run the University all by themselves.[12]

The ultimate statement in a Board document for private and confidential distribution on July 23, 1947, read,

It is with deep regret that in the interest of truth and for the sake of historical accuracy, the facts contained in this memorandum had to be recorded.

There was an abrupt change of pace in the Bruce household on February 12, 1946 when a letter was received from Florence Amery. Although there had been some communication between the families during the war, it came as a shocking surprise to hear that John, the older son, had been arrested for treason. According to Leo's account, John was a young man who was "...inclined to revolt against the trend of public opinion... and... curiously indifferent to the consequences of his actions."[13] He ran away from school and had several unsuccessful careers. He became a fierce anti-Communist and fascist sympathizer, and when France collapsed he became Vichyite and collaborated with the Nazis. Part of this involved delivering radio broadcasts in Germany which urged peace between Britain and the Nazis. He also tried to recruit a "Legion of St. George" from prisoner-of-war camps with the idea that they would fight with the Nazis against the communists. He denied at his trial that he had ever directly attacked Britain, but stated that he was an avowed anti-Communist.

He was arrested in Italy in 1945 by the British forces on a charge of treason in that he had broadcast on behalf of Hitler and had recruited for the Nazi army. During the trial in London, in October 1945, he pleaded "guilty" to eight charges of treason. It was said the plea was to spare his family.[14] He was convicted and the Home Secretary sentenced him to be hanged for treason. Florence wrote to Angela:

> We found our darling son in the gloomy prison. He had cast off all the hampering things of life through which he struggled for the Truth the Light. He had found both. He shone forth from those grim surroundings sincere, so sincere, in feeling he had done his best against Communism, to him caught and having lived so long in the European revolution of ideas, the greatest of the world's evils. He pleaded guilty, because, he said "They tell me that having fought Communism as I've done, and did all I could to rally anti-Communist forces to save England, and all of Europe I loved, I was fighting an Ally. Hence under the Treason Act of 1351 there is but one sentence." ...His sentence was out of all proportion to that of most others — but he bore no rancour, nor must I... He always wanted big things to do, big causes to fight. He did his best.

His lovely courage is eternal. ...his dear father
said "I am so proud of your courage John, you
are so brave." Like lightning came the answer,
"But I am your son."

To Bruce who had shared Leo Amery's feelings
about Empire and Imperialism and all the other
beliefs that went with the monarchy, it was a tragic
blow. John was executed on December 19, 1945. Leo
said in a brief obituary, "He sleeps well."

But terrible as the tragedy was, there was ironic
good fortune that Herbert Bruce died knowing only
those facts. John had been an avowed anti-Semitic
and had taken part in the general intellectual
pogroms in Europe. In his literature designed to
attract interned British soldiers to the Nazi cause, he
appealed "...in the defence of our homes and children and of all civilization against Asiatic and Jewish
beastility... intend giving the world proof that we are
not all sold off to the Jew and the Plutocrat."

The tragic and terrible irony of Leo's position was
revealed in 1999 by an investigator who searched the
political and personal origins of leading Conservative
politicians. Leo Amery was the son of Elizabeth
Leitner, whose family were Hungarian Jewish scholars, who may have converted to Protestanism. Her
husband, Leo's father, left England after being
divorced. Leo then replaced his legal name from
Moritz and buried his Jewish ancestry. During Leo's
entire life he hid his ethnic origin, although he was a
keen advocate of Zionism with many meetings with
prominent Jewish leaders such as Chaim Weissman,
Arthur Balfour, and V. Jabotinsky.

The poignant history which revolved around
"Racism" and the perceived need in the British social
fabric to conceal certain ancestries forced Amery to
dissimulate in a manner that Bruce could never have

understood or approved. He had committed to tolerance between Christians and Jews, while his close
friend had lived a life that rejected the idea of tolerance, by hiding his origins. But in speculating on
Bruce's reaction to such revelations, it is necessary
to look at the times. Angela, and many others, com-
monly labelled people as "Jews" or "niggers." It was
the norm. It was accepted that Mount Sinai Hospital
in Toronto was founded and erected to give Semites a
place to practice. No Jews were appointed to
University medical staff, and Bruce, for all his tolerance, never challenged at Board meetings the gentle-
man's agreement that one was too many. It was not
until 1954 when Dr. David Bohnen was given an out-
patient appointment that a Jew was appointed to the
U of T Medical Faculty.

* * * * * * * * * * * *

When Massey's term was finished, there was a
renewed activity for replacement. In March of 1953
Arthur Meighen wrote to Bruce that there had been a
movement underway,

> Directed toward my candidacy for the post of
> Chancellor of the Toronto University. I have not
> taken the subject even seriously until today, but
> now I have made up my mind that I would say
> 'Yes' or 'No' not later than Friday evening... I
> would feel better with a letter from you, no mat-
> ter which side it is on, because I know its advice
> would be definitely for my good.

Bruce replied to "Dear Arthur." It appeared that
Phillips had suggested that Bruce was the logical
choice for the next Chancellor and had asked consent
to put his name in nomination. Bruce declined
because of his age and added responsibilities.
"However, Eric would not take no for an answer and

appealed to Angela to try and persuade me on the ground that it would be a nice climax to my career and a fitting reward for 21 years service on the Board... Angela set about to influence me and became enthusiastic and I ultimately capitulated.... ." Bruce had not heard anything further except that Neilly had signed his nomination papers. "You can understand therefore, my surprise at your letter." Bruce immediately sent a telegram to Phillips stating that he would not run against Meighen. "Of course I know you would make an excellent Chancellor and you have my blessing."[16]

This letter crossed one from Phillips to Bruce who stated that four candidates had been nominated for the Chancellorship including Gallie, Dr. R. T. Noble, Dean Beatty, and Meighen.

By the following week it appeared that something had gone awry because Angela wrote a letter to Phillips on April 5:

I wonder if you realize how you have hurt an old friend in me, who was your innocent advocate. There is no need to recapitulate the story of urging Herbert to be nominated for the Chancellorship, saying that both the President and you considered him the logical choice, that it would round out his career etc. etc. To all of which urgings he gave determined refusal. Unfortunately you persuaded me to use my influence, saying how light the duty could be and ultimately I was able to get his reluctant consent, and that largely by doing so, he would keep the post open for you, when you are ready to give up the Chairmanship. When I telephoned the results of my efforts, you were apparently greatly pleased and praised me for what I had accomplished. As for the Chancellorship you will know he never wanted it and he and I are more than thankful that you neglected to put his name up.

The letter was never posted but it was footnoted that: "I saw him personally when he tried to evade responsibilities for his unforgivable neglect in this matter."[17] Apparently Phillips had not put in Bruce's nomination as he was under the impression that Neilly was looking after it.

Bruce recorded that Meighen was not successful and accused "the Board of Governors of double-crossing him." Bruce wrote again, "Dear Arthur: Your defeat was an unfortunate thing for the University as you would have brought great distinction to the office of Chancellor. ...The Academic people wanted to honour someone more intimately connected with the work of the University and therefore decided to support Beatty."

Samuel Beatty, who had been Dean of the Faculty of Arts since 1936, was a mathematician who enjoyed a wide reputation for his mastery of that science. After being in office he wrote Bruce, in his own hand.

It was very kind of you to let me see the memoranda you kept from time to time on the events leading up to your recall of your consent to stand as a candidate for the office of Chancellor of the University. The outcome is a complete surprise to me, for I have not heard a word of the other man's interest in promoting his own election. After the event, I now wish to say to you that you have the great comfort of knowing that you chose the path of self-denial and generosity touching the interest of a friend.

Beatty then recounted that his nomination had come from a group of students after an informal dinner meeting. He hadn't really given the matter any thought beyond feeling that the "...daily press was doing us all a good turn in trying to interest such a distinguish man as Meighen in the post."

> I assured them that I would do nothing to further my own election and asked them to do the same, beyond arranging for the necessary signatures of graduates before the final date. The outcome was for the most part unexpected, I am sure, but Dr. Gallie told me that it suited him down to the ground. For myself I'm not sure.[18]

Angela, via Bruce, in spite of all the high-powered assistance that was available, was denied this final honour which would have given her great gratification. However, she was able to maintain a unique place at The Wellesley, following her husband's death, when she became the de facto patroness of the hospital and, through great generosity, established the Herbert Bruce Memorial Lectorship.

* * * * *

The joys of being a committed Conservative were tempered by the failings of many of the party leaders to whom Bruce gave his enthusiasm and help. Howard Ferguson was flawed, and his chief motivation became the hereafter of his Ontario office in the High Commissioner's appointment. George Henry embarrassed the Lieutenant-Governor by an improper request to authorize a payment. Manion, an excellent doctor and a fine man, but a poor speaker, failed at the ballot box. Embittered Bennett exited Canada for ennoblement. Meighen was outmaneuvered by King. As a Senator during the Hong Kong affair and the Duff Report he was entreated by Bruce to address the caucus and give leadership to make the most of a poten-

tial Liberal disaster. But Meighen argued that as he was not a caucus member, "...frequent visits to Ottawa and frequent addresses to the caucus"[19] would cause a split between himself and the government party leader. This left Bruce to lead the charge in the House, and although he was effective, it did not bring down the government.

Finally there was Diefenbaker, in whom Bruce found an electible leader, but just at the end of Bruce's political career.

* * * * * * *

Having left the House, Bruce could now give more attention to the University, where he had been a member of the Board of Governors for many years. This gave him an opportunity to continue with his power playing which had been a recurring theme from WW1 onward. Here, in spite of limited success, he drew great satisfaction from the fact that he was helping to shape the future of the major university of Canada.

At that time he relied greatly on a team of fellow thinkers including prestigious business leaders of the province. His choice of friends, who were frequently so busy with their other activities that they gave only partial heed to University problems, was sometimes unfortunate. However, at the worst, the selection was better than when that he picked an enemy. His quarrels with Perley were costly. His difficulties with Hepburn were draining. His disagreements with Frost and other major figures, while demonstrating his independence, frequently led to a poor net result.

For a farm boy, to have realized his deepest wishes was a tribute to his perseverance, his application, and his faith in himself. His climb to many high posts in the nation may well have been because of his ability to make and communicate with friends. While a Methodist mafia gave power to groups, the Anglican affiliation provided opportunity for individual ascendancy. At every turning point in his life Bruce could reach out to a friend or colleague whether it was William Aberhart, Dr. George Adami, Sir Charles Addis, Viscount Alexander of Tunis, Lord Allenby, Lady Nancy Astor, The Earl of Athlone, Sir Allan Aylesworth, Lord Baden-Powell, Honourable Stanley Baldwin, Beverley Baxter, Sir Edward Beatty, Dr. Arthur Beauchesne, Dr. Robert Bensley, Prince Bernhardt, The Earl of Bessborough, J. P. Bickell, Lord Birkenhead, Dr. Claude Bissell, Sir John Bland-Sutton, General Evangeline Booth, John Bracken, Dr. William Brebner, Justice Matthew Cameron, Dr. James Cantlie, Pierre Cardin, C. H. Carlisle, Lady Carnavon, Dr. Alexis Carrell, Neville Chamberlain, Sir John Chancellor, Hector Charlesworth, Sir Winston Churchill, the Duke of Connaught, Dr. George Crile, Dr. Harvey Cushing, Dr. Allan Ryde Dafoe, Lord Dawson of Penn, the Duke of Devonshire, John Diefenbaker, Sir John Eaton, Sir Robert Falconer, G. Ferguson, Dr. J. K. W. Ferguson, Sir Joseph Flavelle, Premier Leslie Frost, Dr. Edward Gallie, Sir Rickman Godlee, Sir Albert Gooderham, Viscount Haymar Greenwood, Dr. Samuel D. Gross, Dr. William Halstead, Richard Burpee Hanson, Dr. J. J. Heagerty, George Henry, Sir Victor Horsley, Cordell Hull, Principal Maurice Hutton, Sir Henry Irving, Dr. Elliott Joslin, Dr. Howard Kelly, Sir Edward Kemp, the Duke of Kent, Sir A. Lane, Sir Wilfred Laurier, David Lloyd-George, Principal James Loudon, Sir Donald Mann, Hart Massey, Raymond Massey, Dr. Charles Mayo, Dr. W. T. G. Morton, Lord Moynihan, Dr. John B. Murphy, Dr. Gordon Murray, Professor A. B. Macallum, Angus Macdonald, Dean J. A. MacFarlane, Ian Mackenzie, H. R. Macmillan, Colonel George Nasmith, Dr. Balmer Neilly, Sir Edmund Osler, Sir William Osler, Sir Henry Pellatt, Sir

George Perley, Charles Power, Dr. Alexander Primrose, Dr. R. A. Reeve, Bishop Robert J. Renison, Dr. W. A. Riddell, Mr. Justice A. Riddell, Thomas Ridout, Lord Salisbury, Sir Ernest Shackleton, Dr. Charles Sherrington, Dr. Sidney Smith, Dr. Clarence Starr, Louis St-Laurent, Dr. Frederick Strange, Dr. Albert Tilley, W. Norman Tilley, Harold Timmins, Lord Tweedsmuir, Norman Urquhart, Sir Edmund Walker, Sir Thomas White, F. Yeats-Brown.

Truly a mighty host on whom he could call for assistance.

Notes

1. Letter, Bruce to Massey, May 9, 1944.
2. Letter, Massey to Bruce, June 24, 1944.
3. Letter, Massey to Bruce, July 22, 1944.
4. Letter, Bruce to Drew, July 22, 1944.
5. Document, "The Election of a Chancellor", July 23, 1947.
6. Letter, Cody to Bruce, August 8, 1944.
7. Transcript, Board of Governors Meeting.
8. Letter, Bruce to Massey, September 12, 1944.
9. Transcript, Board of Governors Meeting.
10. Memorandum, "The Last Scene in the slowly moving farce of the Chancellorship."
11. Private & Confidential Board Document, July 23, 1947.
12. *Financial Post*, April 30, 1947.
13. Rubenstein, W. D. *History Today* 49: 17-23.
14. West, R. *The Meaning of Treason.* 1952: 198.
15. Letter, Meighen to Bruce, March 25, 1953.
16. Letter, Bruce to Meighen, March 28, 1953.
17. Document in Queen's Archives.
18. Document in Queen's Archives.
19. Letter, Meighen to Bruce, June 17, 1942.

The Queen's University Archives, except #13 &14

CHAPTER 15

Epilogue

The rich warm tones of the Processional wandered over the arches of the nave of St. Paul's Church on Bloor Street as a tide of white uniformed nurses flowed down the aisle and the front pews submerged. Herbert Bruce, in his 94th year, mused on the many times he had been present at a graduation of Wellesley nurses. Each remembered year took him back to an absent friend. The major malady of old age is loss of friends. Gone were Hughes, Perley, Caven, Gallie, and dear George McCullagh, drowned in his swimming pool. No longer could Bruce hear Mulock's stringent voice, demanding and congratulating, or his praise after the emergency appendectomy which saved his son's life.

The memories became more vivid as the afternoon sun prismed through the stained-glass windows. The rustling of the starched uniforms, as each graduate walked to the transept to accept her certificate, whispered old names.

What a strange fellow Hepburn had been. Why he had offered me the leadership of a Union Party in the Ontario Legislature! Very unusual! Of course I had considered it for only a day and then wrote back, "I believe that whatever ability that I may have, can be used to best advantage in representing my constituency in the Parliament at Ottawa." It was amazing that the Premier of Ontario in 1942 suggested a coalition government, simply out of spleen against King.

Ah, there goes Nurse Huxley. I remember her mother. She graduated just before the war. Delightful family. Reminds me of that letter from Nurse Gow, who graduated in 1913, when she wrote, "...Dr. Bruce would drive to the hospital after church in a smart, well-groomed span of horses and wearing his church dress, high silk hat and Prince Albert." And over there is Elsie Jones. She graduated in '37, and then became Director of Nursing.

Of course, my life has been filled with delightful families. There have been many happy gatherings, but those friends are all departed. Massey, Manion, Meighen, McMillan, Ross, and Cody. Odd, recalling Cody. He was a good friend, but at the end his ambition to be Chancellor came between us. Pity. It's only an honorary post. Avarice for office drove him. For years I have sat in this pew and listened to his sermons, which taxed my concentration after the first hour. What was it the boys called him — Dr. Dody?

Still, every Sunday morning I bring the grandchildren — Max's two boys — and after the sermon we go home, and Angela serves lunch, and then we play bridge. When David and Herbert were small, they were allowed to put the cards on the floor. They have grown, so quickly, since I pushed their pram around Rosedale.

Bridge. The number of times I have played with Sir William, while he was still here, and now I play at the club on Thursday afternoons. Tragically he outlived his life and I was so sad about that final disaster. But I truly felt that the University would be better with Massey.

There's Miss Puttner. She's an excellent nurse, I've been told. Looks eager and fresh as she steps forward to receive her diploma. I recollect when I got my Certificate in Medicine and now I am the second oldest living Fellow of the Royal College of Surgeons. Think of it. Christopher Heath, who was my chief teacher at University College, London, was a dresser in the Crimean War. The major episode in the Great War was when I objected to sending a Canadian hospital to Gallipoli, when no Canadian soldiers were serving there. The whole principle, for which I campaigned, to have Canadian soldiers cared for by Canadian doctors, was rejected at that time. But I did not gloat when, just before WW2 began, the Minister of National Defence accepted the findings that both "...experience in the last War shows that Canadian sick and wounded prefer to be cared for by their own people and friends, and the value of the morale effect should be taken into consideration." Finally, the recommendations I had made twenty-three years previously were officially accepted!

Max Beaverbrook chortled when I told him that news. He was always my staunch supporter. Imagine, sending me money on my birthday and paying for my Max's education. Beaverbrook has been such a tower of strength, and so successful. Unlike him, I have never really wanted public office. The Lieutenant-Governorship was thrust on me. I did not seek it. Even my election was almost a whim — but I enjoyed being an MP for a short time. And Angela blossomed.

Angela — and those terrible days in France with all the young men from Port Perry who never came back. Where are the boys of the old brigade? The ones I played with in the summer haze? What was it that we used to sing?

> Then teeter-totter holy water,
> Sprinkle the Catholics one by one,

And if this won't do, we'll cut them in two
and bury 'em under the Orange and Blue

I believe that I dozed for a moment, because they are almost at the end of the queue of graduates. What a great day it is for them. Nothing but joy and elation as they prepare to enter their chosen life-work. Many have friends on whom they can count and expect fair play. Well, as I wrote to Meighen in 1952, "I have not very happy memories of my treatment by the Conservative Government. In fact, I have succeeded for the most part in burying the bitterness which I felt for many years for the ruthless treatment given me by my political friends, for whom I gave up a lucrative practice and did a conscientious job and who in turn tried to destroy me. That they did not succeed was not their fault."

It was a relief to my feelings to recount that story to Arthur. Then there was the other matter. I was deeply hurt when my name was crossed off the list to receive a Knighthood by the Director General of Medical Services. Everyone else became a Sir! But maybe that is why Perley offered me a consolation, with the Lieutenant-Governorship of Ontario. But Bennett did it again when he left me off the New Year's Honours' list! And then Phillips forgot to put me on the Chancellor's nomination.

It's a devious world and I have trouble following the motivation of some of my friends. Oh well, in spite of having been called a troublemaker, controversial, non-conformist, and a nuisance, I have enjoyed life. My work, my hospital, my ideals — all have stood fast. Regent Park is a success. There is a health insurance plan. Tolerance has grown and Jew and Gentile can live together. Even Catholics no longer suffer government discrimination. And I enjoyed standing up against my party and voting against that

Family Allowance. That's a fair run for a young boy from Blackstock.

As long as I have had Angela by my side I have been able to weather any rebuff. I have seen joy and discontent but I have been greatly blessed and, as I near the end, I realize that I have attained what Pindar called "the chiefest prize — happiness."

The Recessional gently ended the day, as the stained-glass windows quietly dimmed.

INDEX